This Book Belongs to:

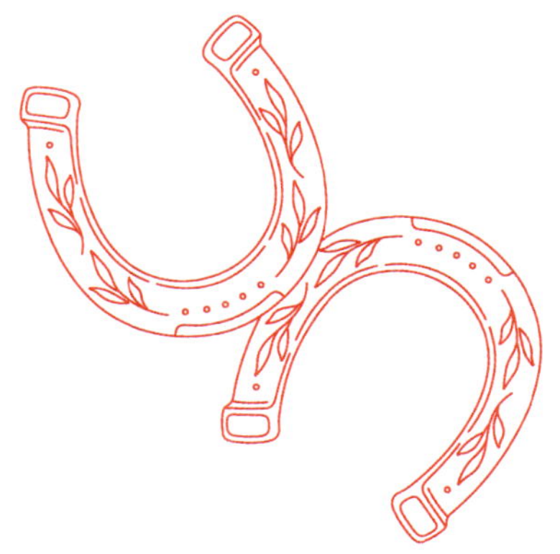

40 DEVOTIONS

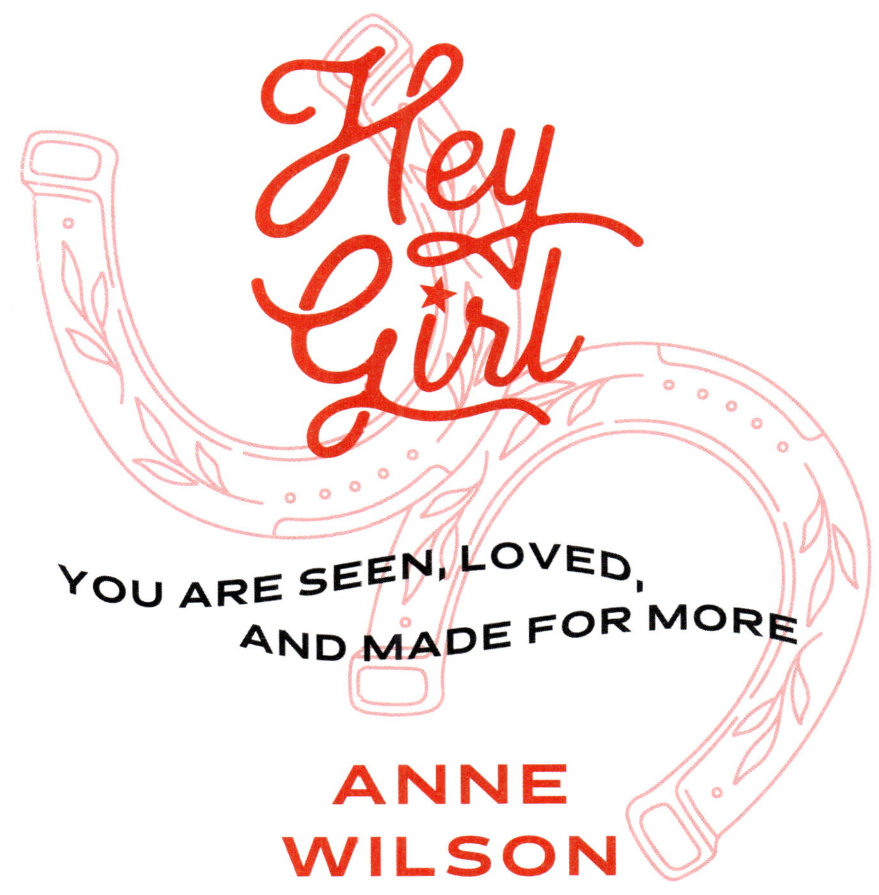

Hey Girl

YOU ARE SEEN, LOVED, AND MADE FOR MORE

ANNE WILSON

Hey Girl: You Are Seen, Loved, and Made for More—40 Devotions

Published by K-LOVE Books, a partner of Forefront Books, Nashville, Tennessee.
Distributed by Simon & Schuster.

Library of Congress Control Number: 2025913099

Print ISBN: 978-1-63763-486-8
E-book ISBN: 978-1-63763-487-5

Cover Design by Greg Jackson, Thinkpen Design
Interior Design by Mary Susan Oleson, Blu Design Concepts

Printed in the United States of America

25 26 27 28 29 30 RR4 10 9 8 7 6 5 4 3

HEY GIRL NATION

Contents

INTRODUCTION

You're Who You're Made to Be

★ ★ ★

Have you ever felt like you're not enough or you don't measure up to those around you? Maybe you feel like you don't meet expectations or have a lot to offer. I've experienced those same feelings. A few years ago I walked through a difficult season. I found myself in the trenches of insecurity and constantly felt like I fell short. I struggled to understand my identity in Jesus and looked for my worth in the opinions of others.

When I was in seventh grade, my mentor, Erica, a godly woman whom I love, spoke over me, "Anne, God sees you as His precious daughter." When she spoke those words, it was like God shifted something in the deepest part of my heart, and the direction of my life changed. I was able to accept and believe the truth, that I am God's precious daughter. I am a daughter of the most high King. I don't belong to the world or the enemy—I belong to Jesus. That was such a turning point for me. God lifted the burden of pleasing everyone and being what others wanted me to be. I just had to be Anne, God's precious daughter. He would help me do everything He had planned for me. Wow! What an amazing truth.

Over the past five years, God has blessed me with an incredible opportunity to travel the country as a music artist and write songs. I cannot believe the doors He has opened! But my greatest honor and deepest security is knowing that I'm a child of God. Whatever I accomplish in my lifetime, my biggest achievement is simply being His beloved daughter.

The song "Hey Girl" was birthed out of that heart. When we walk in the truth that God loves us and wants to have a relationship with us, it puts everything else into perspective. It has been my joy and privilege to sing that song at my concerts and encourage girls and women to embrace their identity in Christ.

A few years ago the online community "Hey Girl Nation" was created to spread that message and remind young women of their worth in Him. Our goal is to provide a positive message to the next generation and show that incredible things happen when women fix their eyes on Jesus.

The second I take my eyes off Him my insecurities and anxieties flare up. Everything I struggle with becomes bigger and scarier when I try to take control. But when I hand over the control to my Jesus, I gain a heavenly perspective. He always has a good plan and provides for all my needs—even those I don't know I have. He invites me to rest in Him.

Matthew 11:28 says, "Come to me, all you who are weary and burdened, and I will give you rest."

I'll never forget the day I wrote "Hey Girl." The song was so special to my heart because I knew God was going to do so much through it. I remember thinking, *If this song helps just one girl get through her struggles, it's worth it.* We released it as a radio single and produced a music video featuring regular girls and women. One hundred girls from all over the nation came to be part of it—some of them dear friends and family members. Even the producer was a woman! The video highlighted how special women are to the Lord. God loves His daughters, and they have incredible value in His kingdom.

I'm so grateful God used that moment to inspire the song and the movement. I have a heart for people walking through heartache. I want to remind women of how much Jesus loves them.

In this devotional I want to have some important conversations about what God's Word says regarding identity, beauty, friendship, faith, victory, and more. If you feel like you're not enough, I want to remind you that your greatest treasure—the truth that defines you—is that you are a blood-bought child of the King. The same God who created the universe created you. He is with you and promises to help you overcome any challenge that comes your way. I go to bed every night thanking God that I'm His child. When you know you're His girl, you can face life with courage and grace. You are His precious daughter! Always remember: You're who you're made to be.

—Anne

SECTION ONE

Messin' with Your Mind

Do not conform to the
pattern of this world,
but be transformed by the
renewing of your mind.
Then you will be able to test
and approve what God's will is—
his good, pleasing and perfect will.

—Romans 12:2

The enemy is crafty. He knows just how to whisper lies that sound true.

YOU'RE NOT GOOD ENOUGH.
YOU'LL NEVER CHANGE.
GOD CAN'T LOVE SOMEONE LIKE YOU.

I've heard those lies more times than I can count. But I've learned that just because a thought enters my mind, it doesn't mean it's true. The Bible says that when the enemy lies, he speaks his native language. Satan is a master of fear and confusion, and all his tactics are bent on one thing—taking us down.

That's why we've got to fight back with the truth of God's Word. The enemy wants to mess with our minds and rip us off; he convinces us that something is sweet, but the moment we partake of it, we realize we've been sold a lie that leads to death. God wants to give us good things as He transforms us through renewing our minds. That happens when we stop repeating the enemy's lies and replace them with God's truth about us. We are chosen, forgiven, accepted, and deeply loved.

When lies creep in, we can boldly proclaim the truth—that we are blood-bought daughters of the King! That's how we allow God to rewrite the story in our minds, which leads to changed lives. Learn to recognize the enemy's lies and stand tall, daughter of the King. Let the Father's voice be the loudest one you hear.

DAY 1:

Unveiled Beauty

★ ★ ★

As a teenager I remember hearing hurtful remarks about my appearance. Other girls commented on everything from my weight to my braces to my acne. Their words stung. They couldn't have known the battles I was already fighting: the tears cried in secret, the makeup applied to hide each pimple, the snacks consumed because of the deep grief I was walking through. Feeling ugly only increased my pain.

I'm guessing you've experienced something similar. Maybe it's not your skin or weight, but something else about you that makes you want to hide. Something that makes you believe you're not enough. For years I tried exterior "solutions"—skincare regimens, healthy eating plans, exercise—but no matter how much outward change I sought, nothing fixed the way I felt inside.

If I could fix my imperfections, I'd feel beautiful and confident. Or so I believed. I love the words of Psalm 34:5, which say, "Those who look to Him are radiant; their faces are never covered with shame." That verse didn't feel true for me for a long time. I was aware of every blemish or extra pound. But the Lord was faithful to not simply "fix" my skin or give me the figure I wanted, but to start with "heart surgery."

As my relationship with God has grown, He's been teaching me the truth about my outward appearance—that my worth is not tied to how I look. I was intentionally designed by God to look like this—flaws and all. God wasn't waiting for me to have clear skin or be a certain weight before He used me. He was already at work—using me just the way I was.

That's what it means to live in authenticity—choosing not to hide behind our fear of what others think. Even in our imperfections, we reflect His glory.

Listen to the words of 2 Corinthians 3:18: "And we all, who with unveiled faces contemplate the Lord's glory, are being transformed into his image with ever-increasing glory, which comes from the Lord, who is the Spirit."

As we look directly to Jesus, we are being transformed into His image through His Spirit. Jesus wasn't considered good-looking by the world's standards. Isaiah 53:2 says, "He had no beauty or majesty to attract us to him." Yet people were drawn to Him and came by the thousands to hear His words and see the glory of God in Him.

What about you? Maybe you're struggling today—wishing you looked different or wondering why God didn't make you with clearer skin or a different shape. Ask God to remind you of who you are. You are a radiant daughter of the King, and He shines through you!

Remember that your sisters out there are going through their own battles and need encouragement. Give someone a compliment today. You never know the difference it might make.

REPEAT AFTER ME:

"God wants to use me just the way I am."

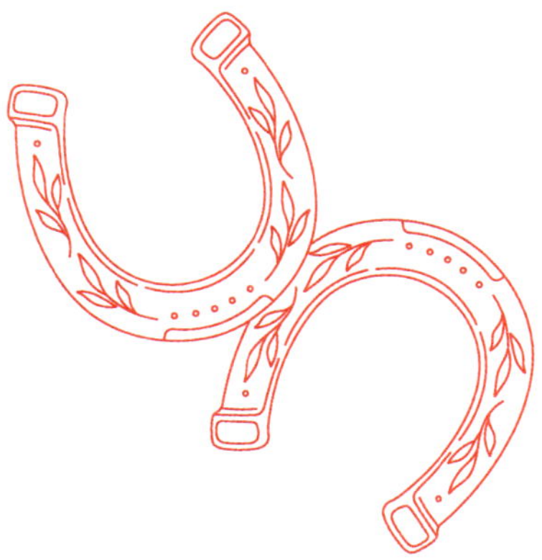

Scripture of the Day:

And we all, who with
unveiled faces contemplate
the Lord's glory,
are being transformed
into his image with
ever-increasing glory,
which comes from
the Lord,
who is the Spirit.

—2 Corinthians 3:18

What are some outward features you've experienced insecurity or shame about?

Invite Jesus to take away those insecurities and remind you of your beauty as His daughter. There is only one you! How might God use you now to bless others and spread His message of hope? List one idea (examples: volunteering at church, leading a Bible study with friends, encouraging someone at school).

You are so valuable to your heavenly Father. Ask Him to fill you with His love and joy today.

Hey, Girl! Let's Talk to God

Dear Radiant Lord,

Thank You for removing my shame when I look to You. Help me to live radiantly with an unveiled face, trusting that You are transforming me into Your likeness. Let Your light shine through me to the people in my life. Use even my insecurities to encourage others and bring You glory. Help me to see myself the way You see me—Your beautiful, beloved daughter.

In Your glorious name, amen.

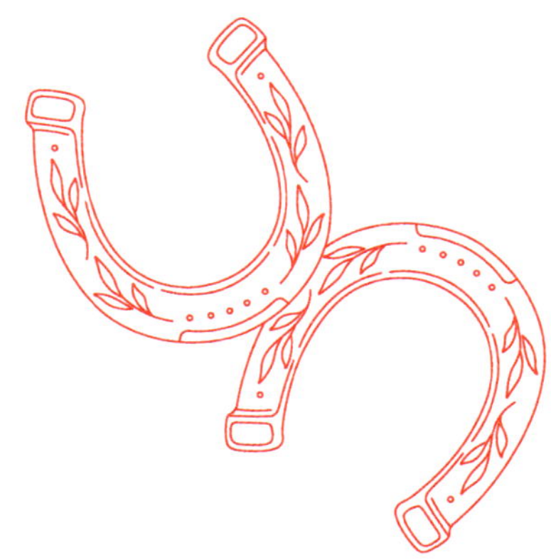

DAY 2:

The Comparison Trap

★ ★ ★

When you look at your reflection in the mirror, what's the first thing you notice? Are you critiquing your appearance and focusing on every flaw? When you look at other girls, what thoughts run through your mind? Are you thinking of all the things they have that you don't? Maybe the faces you see on TV or social media make you feel insecure about your own looks.

Comparison is a trick of the enemy that we all fall for at times. Whether comparing our physical appearances, talents, or our material possessions, contrasting our own situation with someone else's can steal our joy. If I look at all the other talented singers out there, I can get down on myself. Instead of appreciating the amazing qualities God has put into other people, I'm distracted by a feeling that I'm lacking. I compare myself to them and come up short every time. But that's because I was never meant to be them.

One day a sweet and beautiful friend of mine told me she had recently caught herself comparing her appearance to someone else and wasted half her day thinking about all the things she wished she could change. She wished her hair were straight instead of curly and that she could decrease her height by five inches.

Instead of thanking God for the breath in her lungs and the natural beauty He had given her, she found herself stuck in a place of comparison. I've been there, have you? The enemy wants to trap us into believing others have it better than us. The truth is, you and I are lovingly designed by an all-powerful Creator! We are created in Christ's image, the One who is perfect, without any flaws.

Paul talked about this in 2 Corinthians 10:12 (ESV) when he said, "But when they measure themselves by one another and compare themselves with one another, they are without understanding." We frequently fail to understand that God's plan is to use us in our differences to reflect His character more fully. He didn't design us to be the same.

Instead of focusing on what others have or what I lack, God invites me to discover my true identity as I step into the good works He has for me. Y'all, we are servants of the Most High, created by Him in every intricate detail. When we set aside comparison and put our eyes on Jesus, we will see our insecure thoughts begin to fade. The One who made you tells you what you're worth, and no one can take that away.

REPEAT AFTER ME:

"I am designed by a loving, all-powerful Creator!"

Scripture of the Day:

Let us run with
perseverance the race
marked out for us,
fixing our eyes on Jesus, the
pioneer and perfecter of faith.
For the joy set before him he
endured the cross, scorning its
shame, and sat down at the right
hand of the throne of God.

—Hebrews 12:1–2

What gifts has the Lord given you?

How can you use these gifts to glorify the Lord and help build His kingdom?

What scriptures can you memorize this week as your personal battle cry to combat lies the enemy tells you?

Hey, Girl! Let's Talk to God

Lord,

Thank You for creating me in every intricate detail. Help me to appreciate all You've given me. You know I sometimes fall into the trap of comparison—feeling that others have it better than I do or that I lack something. When I feel that way, remind me of the truth that I am created by You to reflect Jesus in this world. Help me see the beauty of Your plan unfold in my life and appreciate all You've blessed me with. I pray I would see how You're working in other people's lives, too, and celebrate their victories. Help me set my eyes on You, Jesus.

In Your glorious name, amen.

DAY 3:

Battling the Inner Voice

★ ★ ★

Have you ever noticed that sometimes the hardest voice to silence is the one inside your head? Growing up, I didn't think I had a good voice. (I also had terrible stage fright—so the thought of doing anything on a stage was terrifying!) I didn't think I had a lot to offer. As I entered junior high and high school, that feeling only deepened.

Then I was asked to sing at my brother Jacob's funeral. That day, as I sat at the piano, singing a worship song to Jesus, He began to change my heart. God gave me a vision, though it was small and a little blurry, of how I could use singing to spread the gospel and give people hope. Even though I felt the calling, the voice inside my head didn't go away. It whispered,

You're not strong enough.

You're too broken, why do you think you can do this?

God could never use someone like you.

Maybe you've heard a similar voice. After losing Jacob, the grief and sorrow I felt nearly drowned out everything else. I found myself believing the lie that healing was impossible and I'd never feel joy again. I also battled the usual teen insecurities about my appearance. I would say cruel things about myself—to myself—that I would *never* say to another person. Maybe you've experienced that too.

But in the middle of my pain and inner thoughts, I heard another voice. That voice was gentle and quiet, and reminded me of who I am in Christ. A verse that has been an encouragement to me is Psalm 19:14: "May these words of my mouth and this meditation of my heart be pleasing in your sight, LORD."

The words we speak out loud matter, but what we say to ourselves in quiet moments can affect us even more. The meditation of our hearts directly influences what we believe and who we put our trust in. I can be my own worst critic. If I don't hand over the negative thoughts to Jesus, the enemy is more than happy to take the mic.

The good news is that Jesus wants to renew our minds so we can see ourselves as He does—as His precious daughters. When I start replacing the lies with God's truth, something shifts. Instead of saying, "I'm not good enough," I repeat to myself, "I am fearfully and wonderfully made" (Ps. 139:14). Instead of accepting the belief that God can't use me, I claim this truth, "His power is made perfect in my weakness" (2 Cor. 12:9, my paraphrase). And rather than believing that I'm not strong, I boldly say, "I can do all things through Christ who gives me strength!" (Phil. 4:13, my paraphrase).

If your inner voice is trying to convince you that you're worthless, I'm here to tell you you're not alone. But you don't have to listen! Let God and His Word speak truth over you. Let the voice of the One who created you be louder than the lies the enemy is telling you. You are His chosen, beloved daughter. You are enough. There is only one you. You're who you're made to be! Don't ever forget that.

REPEAT AFTER ME:

"No matter what my inner voice tells me, I am a chosen, beloved daughter of the King."

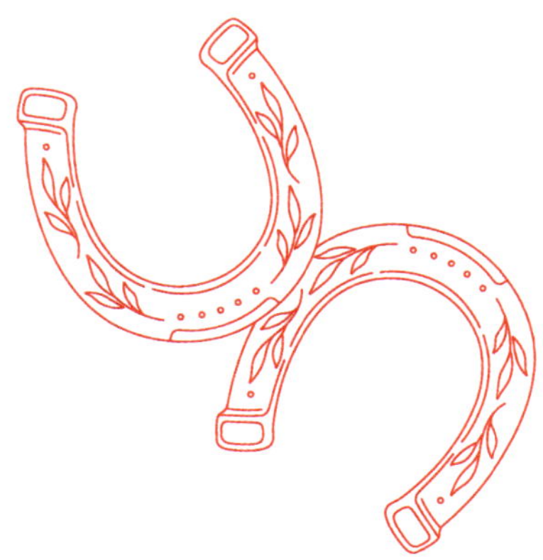

Scripture of the Day:

May these words
of my mouth and
this meditation
of my heart
be pleasing
in your sight,
Lord, my Rock
and my Redeemer.

—Psalm 19:14

Note to Self

One way to override the lies we tell ourselves is to discover what the faulty messages are (for example, "I'm not enough," "I'm worthless," "I can never change," "Others are better than me"). What are the lies you speak to yourself?

Do an online search or use the index in your Bible to find a verse that combats each lie. (Example: Lie: "I'm not good enough." Verse: Psalm 139:14 says, "I am fearfully and wonderfully made.")

Lie 1:

Verse/truth:

Lie 2:

Verse/truth:

Lie 3:

Verse/truth:

Spend a few moments praying or journaling, asking God to renew your mind as He banishes the lies and reinforces His truth on your heart. If you've been agreeing with these lies for a while, it's going to take some time to replace them. Mark this page and revisit it every morning, so you can start your day in the truth of who you are!

Hey, Girl! Let's Talk to God

Lord,

Sometimes my thoughts feel heavy and defeating. When I'm feeling down on myself, help me to tune into Your voice of truth. I pray the words of my mouth *and* the meditations of my heart—even about myself—would be pleasing to You. Remind me of who I am in You—chosen, loved, strong, enough. Write Your truth on my heart so I can live for You and be everything You've created me to be, my Jesus.

In Your glorious name, amen.

DAY 4:

Living in Love

★ ★ ★

What makes you feel loved? I feel loved when my mama spends time with me and pours encouragement into me. I feel loved when my daddy embraces me and calls me "Princess." I feel loved when my dog Annie Oakley smothers me with sweet puppy kisses. Each of us was designed to love and be loved. Not only is love God's idea—*He is love.*

Listen to what Paul said about love in Ephesians 3:17–19: "I pray that you, being rooted and established in love, may have power, together with all the Lord's holy people, to grasp how wide and long and high and deep is the love of Christ, and to know this love that surpasses knowledge—that you may be filled to the measure of all the fullness of God."

As followers of Jesus, we are to be "rooted" in Christ's love. That means that everything we do, every attitude, every conversation or interaction, is motivated by love. It means that we pull our nourishment and strength from love and that God's love is what anchors us. That can be difficult in a world that promotes self-gratification, where anything and everything we want is at our fingertips. But these things—apart from God's love—will only make us feel emptier. The way to be rooted in God's love is to remind yourself daily of how much He loves you and to spend time in His presence, letting Him love you right where you are.

Maybe you're struggling to feel His love...or to feel love at all. We have an enemy who lies to us and tries to tell us we're worthless and unlovable. But the love God has for you is overflowing and never-ending. It is better than the love of any human (or precious pup!) and cannot be expressed in words.

God knew you before you were born and knows the number of hairs on your head. Jesus gave His life for you. When you know—*really* know—God's love deep in your soul, you will naturally be a more loving person. God's love always multiplies. The more loved we feel, the more love we'll show to others. Consider how the knowledge of God's amazing love might change how you live today.

REPEAT AFTER ME:

"I am loved by God with an everlasting love."

Scripture of the Day:

The Lord appeared to us
in the past, saying:
"I have loved you with
an everlasting love;
I have drawn you
with unfailing kindness."

—Jeremiah 31:3

Beloved, if God so
loved us, we also ought
to love one another.

—1 John 4:11 ESV

What makes you feel loved (sweet gestures from loved ones, gifts, kind words, etc.)?

What makes you feel God's love?

How did Paul describe love in Ephesians 3:17–19? What difference can it make in your life?

What are some ways you can show God's love to others?

Hey, Girl! Let's Talk to God

Dear Loving, Heavenly Father,

Thank You for loving me! I may not always feel Your love, but I know it is there. Please remind me of the many ways You care for me each day. Thank You for showing Your love by sending Your Son to die a painful death on a cross and rise again so that my sins could be forgiven. I praise You for creating me and giving me hope and a purpose. Thank You that there is nothing I can do (or *not* do) that will change Your love for me. I love You, Lord. I believe that You love me. I choose to open my heart to You and let Your perfect love in. Help me to experience Your love more and to love You more in return. [Spend a few moments in His love here, sweet sister. Close your eyes and try to imagine you are wrapped in His arms. Relax there and breathe. You are safe and loved.]

In Jesus' precious name, amen

DAY 5:

The God Who Gives Us Peace

★ ★ ★

Fear wasn't something I struggled with as a kid. I was the girl who could sleep through a storm, and I wasn't afraid of the dark. I boldly followed my brother into all kinds of crazy (and mildly dangerous) adventures. But after Jacob died, something shifted. Anxiety pushed in through the wounded places of my heart and seemed to take over. I couldn't eat. I couldn't sleep. Some days I couldn't even seem to catch my breath.

I later learned these experiences were completely normal for someone who had experienced trauma. My body and nervous system were doing all they could to help me regulate after a painful experience. The anxiety seemed to come in waves. Between each one, I could catch my breath and remember God was still with me.

Those moments of peace in the middle of fear were proof that God was with me. He holds us when it feels like everything is falling apart. Maybe you've been through something painful or frightening too—a loved one's cancer, a scary accident, or an unexpected tragedy. It's okay to feel afraid. We read about many people in the Bible who had moments of fear.

The Gospel of Matthew tells a story about a time when Jesus' disciples were terrified (8:24–27). They were out on a boat, and without warning a violent storm came up on the lake. Waves swept over their vessel, and they thought they were about to die. Scripture tells us that Jesus was sleeping. Overcome with terror, the disciples woke Him and said, "Lord, save us! We're going to drown!"

Jesus answered them, saying, "You of little faith, why are you so afraid?" (v. 26). Then He spoke to the winds and the waves, and the lake became calm.

The disciples were amazed. They asked, "What kind of man is this? Even the winds and the waves obey him!" (v. 27).

My life felt like that storm. In my grief over losing Jacob, performing the basic functions of living felt like waves sweeping over me. Little by little, God began helping me see the truth: The storm and the waves did not have the power to destroy me because they were obedient to Christ.

Every challenge, each wave of pain, was an opportunity to choose trust. When I allowed Jesus, who ruled the storm, to rule my heart, fear began to lose its power over me.

Psalm 56:3 says, "When I am afraid, I put my trust in you." Fear will come, but Jesus is our solid anchor through life's storms. Fear doesn't have to define my story. Jesus does.

If you're struggling with worry or anxiety in your life right now, you're not alone. In this broken world, fear and worry will come. But they will also leave, and it's God's perfect love that drives them out. If you find your anxiety getting out of control, talk to a trusted adult; I had a counselor help me to walk through my grief. Then give your anxiety to Jesus. He is big enough for your hurt, strong enough for your fear, and gentle enough to carry your heart through the biggest storms.

REPEAT AFTER ME:

"Jesus is stronger than my fear."

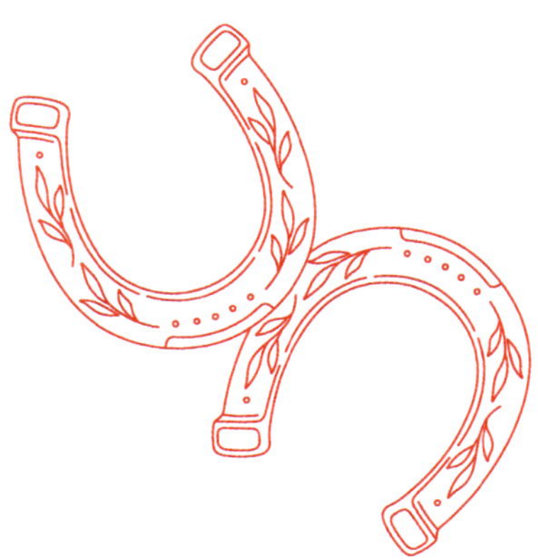

Scripture of the Day:

Do not be anxious
about anything,
but in every situation,
by prayer and petition,
with thanksgiving,
present your
requests to God.

—Philippians 4:6

Note to Self

Think of something you feel anxious about and write it down in the chart below. Maybe it's a challenge you're facing or something going on in your family. For the next five days, pray about it, asking God to give you peace and whatever else you need. Circle how you feel each day—0 being not-at-all anxious and 10 being extremely anxious.

The thing making me anxious is

Today's Date:	I feel:
______________________	0 1 2 3 4 5 6 7 8 9 10
______________________	0 1 2 3 4 5 6 7 8 9 10
______________________	0 1 2 3 4 5 6 7 8 9 10
______________________	0 1 2 3 4 5 6 7 8 9 10
______________________	0 1 2 3 4 5 6 7 8 9 10

No matter what you're going through, remember God is with you. Memorize Psalm 56:3: "When I am afraid, I put my trust in you." Write it on a card and post it somewhere you'll see it each day.

Hey, Girl! Let's Talk to God

Powerful God,

I confess that sometimes fear overwhelms me. When circumstances feel scary, I don't always know how to trust You. But I know You are my anchor in the storm. Thank You for the peace You provide when I feel tossed by the wind and waves. Help me to rest in Your powerful presence, knowing You're big enough for all I'm feeling. Give me wise people in my life who can help me navigate rough waters. Remind me I'm never alone, and that You are always in control.

Amen

SECTION TWO

What You're Worth

Because of his great love for us, God,
who is rich in mercy, made us alive with Christ
even when we were dead in transgressions—it is by grace
you have been saved. And God raised us up with Christ
and seated us with him in the heavenly realms in
Christ Jesus, in order that in the coming ages
he might show the incomparable riches of his grace,
expressed in his kindness to us in Christ Jesus.

—Ephesians 2:4–7

Have you ever felt like the world is trying to put a price tag on you based on your looks, status, or performance? Sometimes it feels like everybody and their mother has an opinion about you, doesn't it? Let me remind you of something: You are priceless to God. He created you and He sent His only Son to die for you. Your value isn't found in how you look, your talents, or your popularity. It's found in the God who loves you and showed that love through Jesus.

God not only saved you; He also raised you up and seated you with Jesus in the heavenly realms. That's how valuable you are to Him! You're not just surviving down here on earth; you've been given a place of honor in heaven.

So when the world tries to tell you you're not enough, remember the truth: The God of the universe thought you were worth the cross. Hold on to that fact and let it shape how you see yourself. Because you, sweet girl, are treasured, chosen, and deeply loved by your heavenly Father.

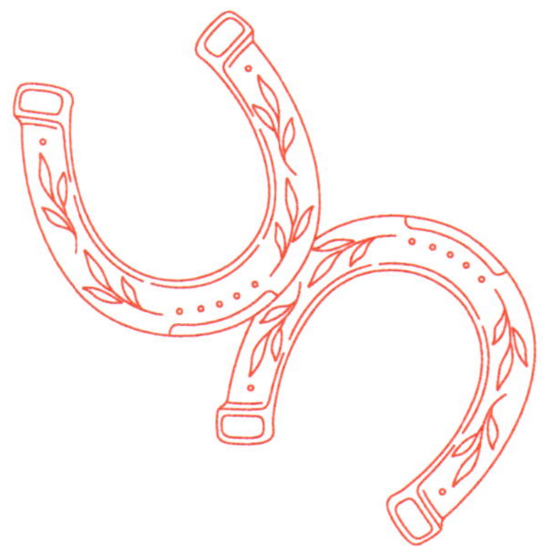

DAY 6:

Crazy Kind of Beautiful

★ ★ ★

Nothing makes me feel more beautiful than slipping into a dress designed by my sister and pulling on a pair of sparkly cowboy boots. I seem to walk taller, and my smile shines brighter.

What makes you feel beautiful?

When I'm on tour, I see a variety of beautiful women, young and old, at my concerts. I'm always amazed by God's creativity! Curly hair and straight; an array of skin tones; freckles, birthmarks, and my favorite—an assortment of amazing smiles!

Even surrounded by such obvious beauty, I know that many of those stunning women struggle to feel beautiful at times. I do. Instead of recognizing all the ways God has made us beautiful, we fixate on our flaws.

In Psalm 139:14 the psalmist proclaimed, "I praise you because I am fearfully and wonderfully made; your works are wonderful, I know that full well." One way we as women can embrace our God-given beauty is to recognize the nature of our Creator—He makes exquisite things! He dots the hillsides with wildflowers. He meticulously designs the pattern of each sparkling snowflake. He crafts tiny, intricate babies inside their mother's womb.

Regardless of my height, weight, hair color, and other features, I was purposefully designed by a God whose works are wonderful! Many of us are tempted to judge our bodies based on how we measure up to the standard of beauty we see on our screens. We equate "beauty" with certain external attributes—shiny hair, a certain body type, or a particular skin tone. What might change if you began to praise God for creating you exactly as you are? What would happen if you acknowledged that all His works are wonderful, including *you*?

I have always loved the story of Amy Carmichael. As a child growing up in Ireland, she disliked her plain brown eyes and pleaded with the Lord to give her the beautiful blue eyes she desired. When Amy grew up, she became a missionary in India, doing important work in a country where the population didn't look like her. It was then that Amy recognized God's wisdom in giving her brown eyes. Staining her skin with coffee, she was able to go to Hindu temples undetected and rescue young girls who had been abandoned there, destined for lives of slavery or prostitution. Without her brown eyes, Amy would not have been able to fulfill the life-saving mission God had given her. During her ministry in India, Amy helped countless children.

Amy is just one example of God's intentional design of our bodies and physical appearance. Each one of us is beautiful in His eyes, exactly the way He created us. Our unique blend of features has purpose. Take some time today to thank God for lovingly creating you for His glory. When He looks at you, He sees a crazy kind of beauty this world can never explain. Praise Him for making beautiful things—including you!

REPEAT AFTER ME:

"I am fearfully and wonderfully made!"

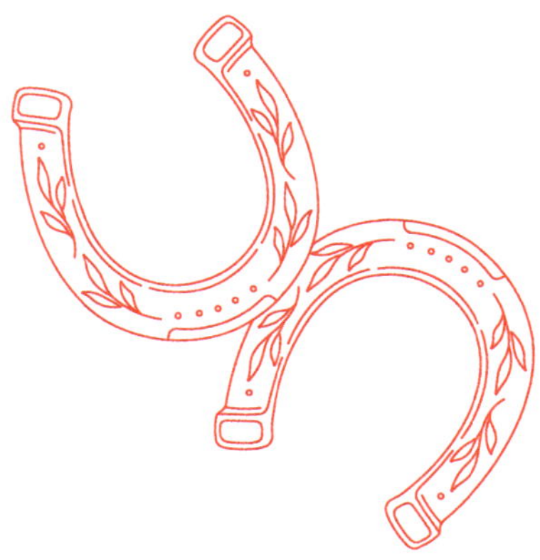

Scripture of the Day:

You are
altogether
beautiful,
my darling;
there is
no flaw in you.

—Song of Songs 4:7

Note to Self

List three things that make you feel beautiful (mine are a cute dress and boots!):

1.

2.

3.

What are some things you love about your outward appearance? (List at least two!)

Hey, Girl! Let's Talk to God

Write a prayer, thanking God for His wonderful works in creating you!

Dear Mighty Creator,

Thank You for

I worship You for

When I'm struggling to feel beautiful, remind me of the truth that I am Your daughter. I ask for help to see myself as You do. I love You because

I praise You because I am fearfully and wonderfully made!

In Jesus' glorious name, amen.

DAY 7:

Inside-Out Beauty

★ ★ ★

When I think of the word *beautiful*, I think of my mama. She's lovely on the outside, of course, but what is most stunning is her beautiful character. She's strong. She loves fiercely. She prays tirelessly. She loves Jesus (and me). She gives and gives without asking for anything in return. That kind of beauty never fades—it only grows as the years pass.

First Peter 3:3–4 tells us where true beauty comes from: "Your beauty should not come from outward adornment, such as elaborate hairstyles and the wearing of gold jewelry or fine clothes. Rather, it should be that of your inner self, the unfading beauty of a gentle and quiet spirit, which is of great worth in God's sight."

The world tries to convince us that beauty is all about what's on the outside—how we look, the clothes we wear, or how we present ourselves. But God looks straight into the heart. When the prophet Samuel was anointing the next king of Israel, he quickly noticed Jesse's impressive oldest son. But God told him: "Do not consider his appearance or his height, for I have rejected him. The Lord does not look at the things people look at. People look at the outward appearance, but the Lord looks at the heart" (1 Sam. 16:7). The youngest brother, David, a shepherd, would be the next king.

It's true that people look at one's outward appearance. I've been guilty of judging a book by its cover—have you? There's nothing wrong with wanting to look your best. But when God turns His eyes on us, He sees what others don't. He sees our character—inner beauty that grows as we follow Jesus and are transformed into His image.

I'm so grateful to have so many examples of beautiful women in my life—my mom, my sister, friends, mentors. Think of the beautiful women in your life—those who love Jesus and others deeply. What makes them most attractive? As you spend time with the Lord, reading His Word, praying, and serving others, you are growing in beauty too.

Let the godly women in your life inspire you to press into your relationship with Jesus and grow in the grace and knowledge of Him. The world might not always recognize that kind of beauty, but God does. And that kind of lasting beauty changes lives.

REPEAT AFTER ME:

"I am growing in inner beauty that reflects a beautiful God."

Scripture of the Day:

Charm is
deceptive, and
beauty is fleeting;
but a woman
who fears the Lord
is to be praised.

—Proverbs 31:30

Make a list of some of the beautiful women in your life. What internal qualities make them beautiful?

Now list some inner qualities that make *you* beautiful (desire to serve others, humility, kindness, etc.):

Write a note of encouragement to a beautiful woman you admire. Mail it or deliver it this week.

Hey, Girl! Let's Talk to God

Beautiful God,

This world sends me so many messages about what I should look like and how I should dress to be accepted and valued. It seems everyone wants to tell me what I'm worth. But I have decided to let You tell me my worth. Lord, remind me of what You find beautiful—a gentle, quiet spirit that desires to serve You and bless others. Thank You for the gift of the godly women in my life who show me what true beauty looks like. Help me be a woman of character who is growing in You and radiates Your beauty to the world. When others look at me, may they see more and more of You.

Amen

DAY 8:

Beauty in the Details

★ ★ ★

I have always loved immersing myself in the beauty of God's creation. Whether hiking up the hill on Grandad's farm, watching a sunset at the beach, or listening to the wind blow through the trees in a forest, I seem to feel more connected to God when I'm surrounded by the beauty of His creation.

A few years ago, my sister, Elizabeth, and I began to dream about a photo shoot in the mountains for my *Rebel* album. Elizabeth is an amazingly creative person who has always been an advocate of my dreams. We created a Pinterest board with pictures and ideas that added up to a vision that was bold and full of beauty. I wanted the shoot to take place in a setting that captured the heart of what it means to be a rebel follower of Jesus. Following Jesus is like a wild adventure into the unknown filled with rare beauty and unexpected discoveries. At times you must forge ahead on the rugged path when others are choosing the easier road.

Many months later, God graciously brought that dream to life. Nestled in the valley between the Gros Ventre and Teton mountain ranges, Jackson Hole, Wyoming, provided the stunning backdrop for what would become my album cover. During the shoot we stayed on a quiet ranch unplugged from the world. With no phone service or outside distractions, I was blown away by the beauty of God's creation.

On the last day of the shoot, we were at the base of the Grand Tetons with a female park ranger when we saw a herd of bison migrating. We all had to stop and just watch, allowing the herd to move on. In that divine delay I heard the Lord saying, *Pause and see My majesty, Anne. Nothing is too difficult for Me.*

I'll never forget what I felt standing in front of those mountains. I was reminded of the words of Psalm 104:24: "How many are your works, Lord! In wisdom you made them all; the earth is full of your creatures." God's majesty in creation through a herd of bison inspired me. Following Jesus makes you a rebel in this world. At times it may feel like you're swimming upstream. Like nature, the journey is wild and bold and sometimes unpredictable. God asks you to stand firm in the truth, even when those around you don't.

When we got that perfect photo for the album cover, I thought about how God reveals Himself through His beautiful world. Even small creatures—a mountain goat, a croaking frog, a starfish in a tide pool—declare God's glory. How much more is His glory shown through us and the story of redemption! First Peter 1:12 tells us that when it comes to the gospel, "even angels long to look into these things."

How has God met you and inspired you through His creation? Next time you're in a beautiful setting, pause to notice what He has made. Walk outside and look around; bend down to examine a tiny blade of grass; stare off into the horizon; listen to the birds singing. Thank God that He made this all for you. If He can make all this and keep it working day after day for thousands of years, He can take care of you too. If you're ever wondering what you're worth, remember that out of all that He created, you are His most loved and valued possession.

REPEAT AFTER ME:

"Out of the many beautiful things God created,
I am His most loved and valued possession."

Scripture of the Day:

Are not two sparrows
sold for a penny?
Yet not one of them
will fall to the ground outside
your Father's care.
And even the very hairs of
your head are all numbered.
So don't be afraid;
you are worth more
than many sparrows.

—Matthew 10:29–31

Note to Self

Choose one of the following activities to connect with God through nature:

- Take a nature walk or plan a trip to get out into God's creation. Spend some time talking to God and journaling your thoughts. What does He reveal to you as you notice the beauty of the things He has made?

- Create a vision board of a beautiful place you want to visit or parts of creation that inspire you. Print pictures off the internet and glue them to poster board or a large piece of paper. Add a verse about the wonder of God's creation.

- Look up and read Psalm 19:1, Isaiah 40:28, John 1:3, and Revelation 4:11. What do these verses tell you about our amazing Creator?

Hey, Girl! Let's Talk to God

Creator God,

Thank You for the beauty of creation and how it reminds me of Your power and Your love. I see You in the towering mountains and in the gentle breeze. I am in awe of the things You have made and humbled that You care for me. You died for me and rose again so that I could live eternally with You. Jesus, You are beautiful and You create beautiful things. Help me to follow You with my whole heart.

In Your powerful and
glorious name, amen.

DAY 9:

A Priceless Treasure

★ ★ ★

We live in a culture that is hyperfocused on the worth of items—from sunglasses to clothes to cars. We're fascinated by the richest men and women in the world, luxurious lifestyles, and hidden treasures. Some folks go antiquing or thrifting in the hopes of discovering something valuable that has been forgotten.

A dedicated thrift-store shopper in Phoenix, Arizona, struck it rich when he came across a deep-sea diving watch priced at $5.99. The watch happened to be a rare 1959 Jaeger-LeCoultre—one of fewer than one thousand ever made. After purchasing the watch and doing his research, he sold the watch to a collector for $35,000!

I love thrifting, and stories like that inspire me to keep searching for hidden treasures. But the amazing fact is, you and I are worth more than any earthly treasure. Have you ever stopped to wonder what you're worth? Not in the way the world measures worth, but in the eyes of the One who made you? I've wrestled with this question myself. There were seasons when I felt like I had nothing to offer and my past mistakes defined me.

But the Lord gently reminded me, *You are worth everything to Me, Anne.*

In His Word, God declares we are worth His time because He created us and breathed air into our lungs. He tells us we are worth His presence because He desires to be close to us and have a relationship with us. I can't believe that the Creator of the universe desires to spend time with *me*. But it's true.

Even though we've sinned and fallen short, He still calls us worthy because of Jesus. God says we're worth the life of His Son. He gave everything to pay a debt we could never pay. He redeemed us through His sacrifice. Then He gave us the gift of His Holy Spirit, who dwells in us, comforts us, and empowers us to live boldly for His name. He values us enough to equip us for our purpose here on earth—to shine for Him until He returns.

How much do you imagine one minute of God's time is worth? How about one drop of Jesus' precious blood? As priceless as He is, He declares us worth every second of His time…every drop of blood shed.

So the next time everybody and their mother tries to tell you what you're worth, tell them you're a blood-bought, priceless treasure! You were worth creating. You were worth saving. You were worth equipping. Stand tall today, not because you're perfect, but because you're perfectly loved.

REPEAT AFTER ME:

"I am a blood-bought, priceless treasure to God."

Scripture of the Day:

Therefore, as
God's chosen people,
holy and dearly loved,
clothe yourselves
with compassion,
kindness, humility,
gentleness and patience.

—Colossians 3:12

Hey Girl!

Note to Self

What do you think is the most priceless item on earth?

How do you measure your worth on days when you are feeling critical of yourself?

What do you imagine Jesus would say to you if He was looking into your eyes right now?

Hey, Girl! Let's Talk to God

Lord,

Thank You for loving me enough to give everything—Your time, Your presence, and Your life—to bring me back to You. It overwhelms me to know that every drop of blood You shed was because You saw me as a treasure worth dying for. Help me to live like someone who's been bought with that kind of love. Remind me that my identity is not found in the world's approval but in Your sacrifice. Let me walk boldly in that truth and share it with others who need to know how deeply they are loved too.

In Jesus' name, amen.

DAY 10:

The Right Voice

★ ★ ★

Have you ever felt like you weren't enough? Like no matter how hard you tried, you were invisible—or worse, the target of someone else's cruelty? I've talked to so many girls who've carried the weight of rejection on their shoulders, and I've also experienced this burden. Maybe you have too.

People you trusted might have said things that tore into your heart and crushed your spirit. Maybe they talked behind your back or excluded you on purpose. Maybe they told you they didn't want to be friends anymore or made you feel like something was wrong with you.

I've heard stories like this more times than I can count, and the hurt is real. The enemy loves to twist those wounds into lies that stick. *You're not lovable. You're not important. You're not good enough.* But here's what I've learned: Those voices aren't the voice of God. And they don't get the final say over who you are.

Jesus knows what it's like to be rejected. He was betrayed, mocked, and beaten by the very people He came to save. Instead of hardening His heart, He forgave. And He told His disciples to pray for their enemies. Jesus said, "But I tell you, love your enemies and pray for those who persecute you" (Matt. 5:44).

That's so hard to do. Especially when the hurt cuts deep. But when we pray for those who've hurt us, we don't excuse their behavior. We release ourselves from the prison of bitterness. We make space for God to heal the hurt and speak His truth over us. We allow Him to control the situation, not us.

If you're experiencing bullying online or in person, tell a trusted adult. I know from experience that those situations can quickly escalate and lead to anxiety and depression. You shouldn't have to carry that burden alone. Don't ever feel you are stuck in your situation and nothing will ever change. God promises to never leave you, and He uses parents and other wise adults to protect you and help you come up with a plan to leave an unhealthy situation.

Some of you have been carrying around words that were never meant for you. Maybe someone called you stupid or annoying and you believed it. You let those lies make you feel worthless or unlovable. But you are not defined by what others have said about you, sweet girl—*you're defined by what Jesus did for you.*

So allow your loving heavenly Father to replace those lies with truth. He will help you break any agreement you've made with lies of the enemy and take to heart what God says about you. Wherever you are right now, I want you to say this out loud with me (even if it feels weird at first):

I am loved.

I am chosen.

I am not forgotten.

I am fearfully and wonderfully made.

I have purpose.

God is for me.

My past doesn't define me—Jesus does.

I am free.

Let those words soak into your soul. Write them down and post them on your mirror or in your locker. Speak them over your life every day until they drown out the noise of every other voice that tried to tell you otherwise.

Ask God for strength to follow Jesus' example, and pray for the people who hurt you. Ask God to heal their broken places too. Praying for your enemies surrenders them to Christ and makes you free. I've discovered that hurt people hurt people, but loved people love. And, girl—you are deeply, unshakably loved by the One who laid down His life for you.

So walk forward in freedom. Keep your eyes on Jesus, not the crowd. Don't let someone else's rejection keep you from your calling. You are a daughter of the King, and nobody else's opinion can take that away.

REPEAT AFTER ME:

"I am not defined by how others treat me;
I am defined by what Jesus did for me."

Scripture of the Day::

But I tell you,
love your
enemies and pray
for those who
persecute you.

—Matthew 5:44

Note to Self

What are some of the hurtful lies you've believed?

Which statements from the list above resonate with you ("I am loved," "I have purpose," "God is for me," etc.)? On an index card, write down one to three of those statements. Post it on your mirror or put it in your Bible. Speak those words over yourself every day until you really believe them.

If you're facing bullying right now—either online or in person—list two people you can tell. Make a plan to talk to them this week.

1.
2.

My plan is to:

Is there someone who has hurt you who you need to pray for today? Ask God to heal that person's broken places. Surrender that relationship and situation to Him.

Hey, Girl! Let's Talk to God

Creator God,

You see every hurt and every tear. You know every moment I've felt invisible or unworthy. You know the names I've been called and the pain I've carried. Today, I choose to give my pain to You and pray for those who hurt me. I can forgive them because You forgave me first. I trust You to handle this hurtful situation. Heal my pain and help me see myself the way You do. Remind me every day that I am loved and chosen, and that I belong to You. Thank You for calling me by name. I choose to believe Your truth over every lie.

In Your mighty name, amen.

SECTION THREE

Blood Bought Battle Fought

For you know that it was not with perishable things such as silver or gold that you were redeemed from the empty way of life handed down to you from your ancestors, but with the precious blood of Christ, a lamb without blemish or defect.

—1 Peter 1:18–19

Long ago, before you were born, there was a war over your soul. Satan wanted to take you down—to steal, kill, and destroy anything good in your life—but Jesus won. Though the cost was great, the Son of God willingly went to the cross to pay the debt for your sin.

Because of His sacrifice, those who follow Him now walk in freedom and hope. He has redeemed us from an "empty way of life." Our worth isn't tied to our successes or our failures. It isn't dependent on what the world says about us—if we're celebrated or canceled. Our value was set on the cross when Jesus purchased our freedom through His blood.

Some days, life still feels like a battle. We wrestle with insecurities, trials, and the devil's schemes. But every time the enemy whispers lies, we can stand firm knowing Jesus has already fought for us and won. He defeated death and the grave, and we belong to Him. He hears the cries of His daughters and comes to our rescue!

When you feel surrounded by the troubles of life or like the devil is charging at you day after day, be still and let Jesus fight for you. He's already won. Never forget that you are His precious, blood-bought daughter.

DAY 11:

The Cross

★ ★ ★

I used to think I had to be good to earn God's love. This led to frustration because it seemed I could never be good enough. Just when I thought I was making progress, I'd blow up at my sister, say something disrespectful to my mom, or act selfishly toward a friend. It took me a long time to realize that God doesn't love me *more* for my greatest victory or *less* for my biggest mistake. He simply loves me—deeply, endlessly, unconditionally. But that love came with a steep price tag; Jesus paid the price for my rebellion against God.

First Peter 2:24 offers this amazing truth: "'He himself bore our sins' in his body on the cross, so that we might die to sins and live for righteousness; 'by his wounds you have been healed.'"

I wrote a song for my *Rebel* album called "The Cross" that talks about this very thing. (Sidenote: I got to record it with one of my Christian music heroes, Chris Tomlin!) The cross is more than a symbol at church or a cool piece of jewelry. It is the place where everything changed. Jesus suffered and died so that I could be forgiven and spend eternity with

Him. His wounds provided the healing I so desperately needed.

The cross gives us hope in dark places because Jesus didn't stay in the grave. Through His death, He carried the weight of our sin, our sorrow, and our shame...and He overcame. He conquered death, and He is alive!

Maybe you feel unworthy of such a great love. I used to feel that way too. I thought I had to get everything right in my life before I could come to Jesus. Thankfully, the cross tells a different story. There is nothing you or I could ever do that would change God's love for us. We're never too far gone to come to Jesus and receive His forgiveness. Think about the thief on the cross next to Jesus. In faith He asked Jesus to remember him when He came into His kingdom, and Jesus said, "Today you will be with me in paradise" (Luke 23:43).

At the cross, Jesus did something for us that we could never do for ourselves. While we were still sinners, He died for us (Rom. 5:8). Because of Jesus' sacrifice, God invites us to come as we are. We can approach Him right in the middle of our brokenness. God met me in the middle of my greatest heartache and invited me to trust Him. Our questions don't bother God. He can handle them, and He cares enough to have the conversation with us.

Maybe today you feel unworthy or like you've messed up too badly to receive His grace. If you feel distant from God, sweet sister, gaze at the cross. Remember its meaning—Jesus gave His life to free you from sin and shame. Your debt has been paid, you were bought with a price, and you are loved beyond comprehension.

★ ★ ★

REPEAT AFTER ME:

"Jesus gave His life to free me from sin and shame."

Scripture of the Day:

God demonstrates
his own love for
us in this:
While we were
still sinners,
Christ died for us.

—Romans 5:8

Note to Self

Listen to my song "The Cross." Close your eyes and focus on the words. Let God remind you of your worth and the life, forgiveness, and freedom He has provided.

What brokenness or questions do you need to bring to Jesus today? Write a note or draw a picture under the cross. Surrender those things at the foot of the cross. Jesus loves you so much!

Hey, Girl! Let's Talk to God

Write a prayer to God, thanking Him for the cross and His great love for you.

Creator God,

DAY 12:

The Lord Who Fights Your Battles

★ ★ ★

Have you ever had one of those mornings where everything just feels off? Your hair won't cooperate, you burn your breakfast (and your tongue), and you seem to get into a fight with every family member. Sometimes it's not just a bad *day* either—it's a hard *season*. Maybe you're carrying heartbreak no one can see. Maybe you're failing a class, watching someone you love fall apart, losing a friend, or trying to hold it together while everything around you feels like it's crumbling.

Hard seasons are part of life. Sometimes hard seasons are a result of poor choices you or others have made. But sometimes hard seasons come as a direct attack from the one who wants to destroy you and hurt the God who loves you. In fact, Ephesians 6:12 tells us are battles are not "against flesh and blood, but against the rulers, against the authorities, against the powers of this dark world and against the spiritual forces of evil in the heavenly realms." That's intense, y'all! The enemy is real, and an unseen battle rages around us. The true enemy isn't the people who are being mean to you or rejecting you, or the circumstances you face; it's Satan, who hates you and wants to destroy you.

On difficult days, when it feels like everything's going wrong, I sometimes ask myself, *How can I rejoice in a day like this?*

A few summers ago, in my home state of Kentucky, many people experienced devastating floods that displaced them from their homes and neighborhoods. Some folks lost everything—family photographs, favorite clothes, even beloved pets. Because of the powerful and destructive flood waters, some families had no home to return to after nature took its course. It made me wonder: How can we expect them to rejoice when circumstances have brought them to their breaking point? How can *I* rejoice when God gives me more than I feel able to withstand?

There's a story in the Old Testament about four valiant young Jewish men. Daniel, and his friends Shadrach, Meshach, and Abednego, were exiled, stripped of everything familiar, and even renamed to reflect a culture that was trying to erase who they were. Maybe you've felt that too; it can feel like the world is trying to make us forget that God exists and that we are sinful people who need a Savior. Culture tells us we can find alternate ways to be happy and connect with a higher power.

That is the situation Daniel's friends found themselves in when King Nebuchadnezzar commanded that they bow to a golden statue in his likeness. They refused and were thrown into the furnace. But in the fire—literally and spiritually—the three men clung to God. They remembered who they belonged to and believed He would rescue them.

They told the king that their God would deliver them. "But even if he does not, we want you to know...we will not serve your gods or worship the image of gold you have set up" (Dan. 3:18). That is amazing courage. And God came through for them. As they stood in the fire, the king saw a fourth man who looked like the Son of God. It was Jesus!

Maybe your hard season isn't a flood or fire. But whatever you're walking through, the Lord promises to walk with you in it. Whether your best friend is moving away, your parents are getting a divorce, or you're facing mean girls at school, Jesus promises to never leave you or forsake you. When life gives you more than you can handle, remember that God *can* handle it. Even when you can't see it, He is working all things together for your good.

The same God who showed up in the fire with Shadrach, Meshach, and Abednego fights your battles today. He is strong, He is good, and He has a purpose for your life that not even the deepest waters or the hottest flames can take away.

Close your eyes and take a deep breath. Tell yourself: "I'm a battle-fought child of the King." He is with you in every bad day, every broken season, and every step forward.

REPEAT AFTER ME:

"When I am weak, God fights for me."

Scripture of the Day:

God is our refuge and
strength, an ever-present
help in trouble.
Therefore we will not fear,
though the earth give way
and the mountains fall
into the heart of the sea.

—Psalm 46:1–2

What is a battle you have faced or are facing? Where do you see God fighting for you in that battle?

Read Ephesians 6:10–18 about the armor of God. Why do you think He gives you these particular tools for battle?

Which piece of spiritual armor can you focus on today? How will that piece help defeat the enemies you face?

Hey, Girl! Let's Talk to God

Heavenly Father,

Sometimes life is hard, and I don't feel strong enough to face it. Thank You for being my strength when I'm weak. Thank You for fighting for me when the battle rages. Thank You for never leaving my side. Help me to trust that You're working in the middle of difficult days and hard seasons. Teach me to rejoice in this day—not because everything is perfect but because You're still on the throne. I'm so grateful that You've called me Yours.

In Jesus' name, amen.

DAY 13:

Alive in Grace

★ ★ ★

When I was twelve years old, I asked Jesus to be my Savior. In that moment I felt His love so deeply—it was like electricity running through my veins. I'd never felt anything like it before. God's love was real, strong, and personal, and I knew I wanted to follow Him for the rest of my life.

But I quickly learned that following Jesus doesn't mean life gets easy. Doing things God's way would not always be simple, comfortable, or easy. My selfish desires and negative thoughts would trip me up, causing me to feel discouraged and defeated. I'd ask myself, *Why do I still struggle if I've been set free?*

Maybe you've asked yourself that too. You love Jesus, but you still mess up. You still lose your temper, compare yourself to others, or feel like giving up. Sweet sister, I want to remind you of the truth I hold on to: We are not walking this road on our own or in our own strength.

Galatians 5:24–25 says, "Those who belong to Christ Jesus have nailed the passions and desires of their sinful nature to his cross and crucified them there. Since we are living by the Spirit, let us follow the Spirit's leading in every part of our lives" (NLT). That means we don't have to be ruled by our old ways anymore. Those sins and struggles were nailed to the cross with Jesus.

Paul said it even more clearly in Galatians 2:20: "I have been crucified with Christ and I no longer live, but Christ lives in me." That's the heart of the gospel. It's not about us trying harder. It's about Christ living in us—empowering us, renewing us, and guiding us by His Spirit.

The main point of Galatians is that as a believer, I am no longer justified by my ability to perfectly obey the law (think the "Thou shalt nots"). We are not made right with God by keeping a checklist of do's and don'ts. We are made right with Him by grace through faith. God's grace isn't earned—it's a gift. And because He is good, He calls us out of sin into freedom and peace.

What do we do when old attitudes or temptations show up? We lean on the Holy Spirit to give us the power to resist sin and confess it when we fall short. We say, "God, I can't do this on my own, but I trust You to help me." That's what it means to walk by faith. Jesus already won the battle. When He said, "It is finished" (John 19:30), He meant it. Every sin—past, present, and future—was paid in full.

Thanks to Jesus, you and I don't have to carry the weight of trying to be perfect. We are already infinitely loved, specially chosen, and truly free. Keep walking with Him. He paid in full for every sin so that we could know God and walk the joy-filled path of righteousness and peace.

REPEAT AFTER ME:

"Jesus paid in full for my sin, so I can walk in righteousness."

Scripture of the Day:

I have been crucified with Christ
and I no longer live,
but Christ lives in me.
The life I now live in the body,
I live by faith in the Son of God,
who loved me and
gave himself for me.

—GALATIANS 2:20

Note to Self

What "desires of [the] sinful nature" crop up the most in your life (for example, gossip, negativity, disrespect, pride, addiction)?

Write down a few sinful desires you would like to nail to His cross today.

List a few ways you can follow the Spirit's leading today. (Examples: Pray with a friend, read your Bible and journal about what you read, turn on some worship music, avoid situations or people that tempt you to make sinful choices.)

Hey, Girl! Let's Talk to God

Dear Jesus,

Thank You for Your finished work on the cross that sets me free and allows me to stand in Your presence unashamed and beloved. I take my place as Your daughter in that completed work, believing that Jesus suffered and died on the cross, rose again, and ascended into heaven, where He is alive today. Thank You that I don't have to earn my salvation by being "good enough," but that it's a gift of grace through faith. Lord, I don't always measure up. I revert to old patterns that don't reflect You. I pray I would nail the desires of my sinful nature to Your cross and crucify them. Empower me to follow the Spirit's leading in my life. Thank You for the path of holiness You call me to for my own benefit, peace, and joy. I surrender to You completely, Jesus, offering You my heart, soul, and body.

Amen.

DAY 14:

When Peace Is Hard to Find

★ ★ ★

What's the hardest challenge you've faced? When you think about that challenge, does your heart immediately begin to feel the negative emotions of pain, fear, or anger?

Maybe you've had to move to a new city and start over at a new school. Maybe your parents separated, or someone close to you has struggled with addiction or mental health issues. We all fight different battles, but we all know what it's like to hurt and have scars.

I was fifteen when I lost my big brother, Jacob. He wasn't just my sibling—he was one of my best friends. I could always count on his wisdom, and I knew he had my back. Losing him shattered me. I couldn't imagine my life without him in it. For a long time it felt like the cloud of grief might never lift.

During that dark season, the only way I made it through was by clinging to Jesus. Every night, I'd open my journal and write the same words: "Thank You, my Jesus, for getting me through another day." That was all I could offer in my brokenness—surrender. But Jesus met me there.

When Jesus' time on earth was nearing completion, He downloaded some important information on His disciples. He explained the reason for His instructions in John 16:33: "I have told you these things, so that in me you may have peace. In this world you will have trouble. But take heart! I have overcome the world."

Being God, Jesus knew His followers would face persecution for their faith in Him. All of them would be misunderstood and rejected, some of them would face jail time for preaching the gospel, and others would be killed. They had some trials ahead that would threaten to steal their peace. He wanted to encourage them that they could find peace and hope in Him because He would overcome the world through His death and resurrection.

Because He was victorious, no amount of pain, loss, or fear can separate us from His love. When we are crushed under the weight of sorrow, He is the One who carries us. He doesn't promise to take away every hardship, but He promises to walk through it with us—and that gives us peace.

When I've faced trouble in my life, I've found comfort in Jesus' words. He is strong when I am weak, and He lovingly joins me in my sorrow. During stressful events and even tragedy, Jesus gives us peace that is beyond human understanding. That is what I experienced in the days and weeks after I lost Jacob. Many days, I would have had zero peace apart from Jesus. He reassured me with His love. He met me in my sorrow and sheltered me beneath His wing. He gave me enough hope each day to keep going.

Is something stealing your peace today? Jesus knows all your troubles—past, present, and future. He says: "Take heart! I have overcome the world." Try putting your name in that sentence: "Take heart, [insert your name here]! I have overcome the world." No matter what you're walking through, Jesus can calm your anxiety and give you peace. He loves you deeply and walks beside you every step of the way.

REPEAT AFTER ME:

"I can take heart; Jesus has overcome the world."

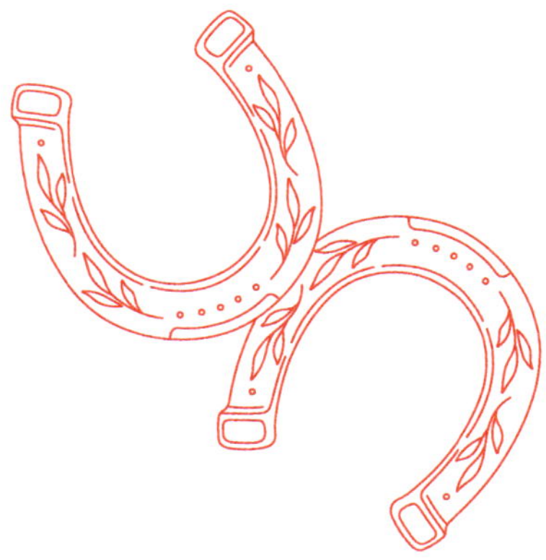

Scripture of the Day:

Peace I leave with you; my peace I give you. I do not give to you as the world gives. Do not let your hearts be troubled and do not be afraid.

—John 14:27

Note to Self

Journaling has helped me get through hard times. Spend some time writing to God about anything stealing your peace. Ask Him to give you what you need to get through today.

Hey, Girl! Let's Talk to God

Prince of Peace,

Thank You for calming my anxious heart. You know every challenge I face and everything that causes me stress and worry. Thank You that I can "take heart" when troubles come my way. Jesus, You have overcome the world through Your perfect sacrifice. I know You can help me overcome anything I'm facing today. I surrender everything and everyone to You again. I give You [insert what you are struggling with today] and release it into Your loving hands. I will trust You with it. Thank You, my Jesus, for walking with me and giving me Your comfort and peace.

In Your powerful name, amen.

DAY 15:

Holy Water Baptized

★ ★ ★

I'll never forget the day I was baptized. I was fourteen, and Pastor Cameron, who had led me to Christ two years earlier, was the one who baptized me. I wore a T-shirt that said "New Life," and that's exactly what I felt I was stepping into. It was this beautiful moment of going under the water, surrendering my old self, and coming up clean.

I knew baptism didn't save me—Jesus had already done that when I gave Him my heart. But it marked a turning point in my faith. My brother, Jacob, was still alive, and I remember his giant grin and the big hug he gave me after I came out of the baptismal. It's a day I'll never forget—the day I declared in front of my family and my church, "I'm following Jesus from here on out."

Baptism is a life-defining moment for a believer. It's our public declaration that our hearts have been transformed and that Jesus is Lord. I love how Romans 6:4 says, "We were therefore buried with him through baptism into death in order that, just as Christ was raised from the dead through the glory of the Father, we too may live a new life."

Through baptism we identify with Jesus' death and resurrection. Going under the water represents dying to our old ways. And when we rise from the water, it symbolizes the new life we now have in Christ. What a powerful picture of redemption and hope. We come as we are, in our mess and imperfection, and allow God's grace to cover us. We're saying, "God, I'm Yours. I want to follow wherever You lead."

Some of Jesus' final instructions to His followers involved baptism. Matthew 28:19–20 says, "Therefore go and make disciples of all nations, baptizing them in the name of the Father and of the Son and of the Holy Spirit, and teaching them to obey everything I have commanded you. And surely I am with you always, to the very end of the age."

If you've never been baptized and you've given your heart to Jesus, I want to encourage you to take that next step. Baptism is a way to honor what Jesus has already done in your heart and the new creation He's shaping you into. It's a declaration to the world that you have entered a new kingdom and new life.

If you've already been baptized, reflect on that special moment. You've been raised to new life. You are a daughter of the Most High King. Let the memory of that day remind you of who you are in Christ.

Jesus died and rose again so we could be free. Baptism is one way we step into all the new life He has for us. So, precious daughter of the King, never forget that you've been made new. You're covered in grace. And you've been raised with Christ to live a life of purpose and hope.

REPEAT AFTER ME:

"Through baptism I publicly proclaim my desire to follow Jesus."

Scripture of the Day:

So in Christ Jesus you are all children of God through faith, for all of you who were baptized into Christ have clothed yourselves with Christ.

—GALATIANS 3:26–27

Note to Self

Read the account of Jesus' baptism in Matthew 3:13–17. What stands out to you in this passage?

Why do you think Jesus needed to / chose to be baptized?

If you have been baptized, write your memories of that day.

Hey, Girl! Let's Talk to God

Jesus,

Thank You for the gift of new life. Thank You for dying on the cross for me and rising again so I could be saved. Help me walk daily in the freedom and identity You've given me. Remind me often of the moment I said yes to You—not just with my heart but with my whole life. Strengthen me to follow You with courage, obedience, and joy.

In Your precious name, amen.

SECTION FOUR

Made-New Child of the King

Therefore, if anyone is in Christ,
the new creation has come:
The old has gone, the new is here!

—2 Corinthians 5:17

When Jesus comes into our lives, everything changes. He doesn't just offer us a fresh start; He makes us brand new. No matter what you've done or where you've been, in Christ you are chosen, loved, forgiven, and free. When He steps into your life, He not only fixes the broken pieces—He transforms you into someone who is completely new!

It's never too late to come to Christ and let Him change you from the inside out. In Him, we can leave behind guilt and shame and walk in the newness of life. As we surrender our lives to Him, Jesus gives us hope and a purpose. The enemy loves to remind us of what we've done and all the reasons we don't deserve God's love, but Jesus reminds us of who we *are*. He knows us inside and out and loves us like crazy! When we say yes to Him, we begin walking in a new identity as a daughter of the King.

Remember that you are a new creation. Step forward with confidence, knowing He's writing a new story through you. A story filled with grace, purpose, and unstoppable love. *You* are a made-new daughter of the King!

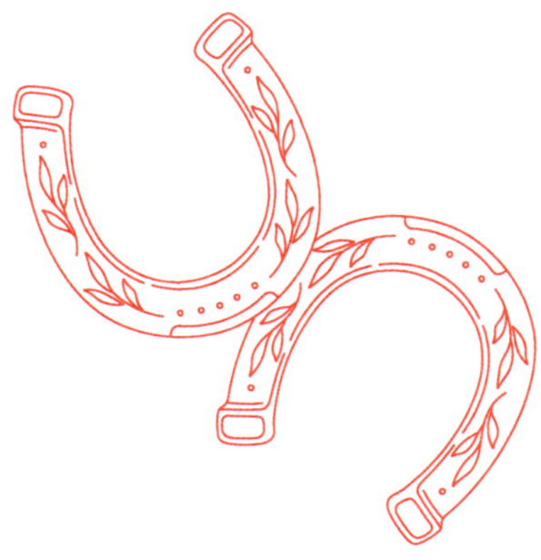

DAY 16:

Hope in Surrender

★ ★ ★

I knelt on the cowhide rug in my Nashville apartment. It was minutes before the song and video of "My Jesus" were to be released. Much like I had done as a twelve-year-old, I surrendered myself to God in the dim lamplight. I surrendered the song—and everything that would come after—into His loving hands. I had no idea what the next steps of my journey as an artist would look like, but I tried to give up my desire to know every detail (a habit Jacob had often challenged me on).

"My Jesus," I prayed, "I surrender to You. I give You today and all the days that follow. Use this song to impact people for the gospel. I release this song to You, God, to do with it what You want. I trust You."

To my amazement "My Jesus" went on to be number one on Billboard's Christian Airplay chart in 2021.[1] God answered my prayer beyond my wildest dreams. He used the song to affect many lives for the gospel and open multiple doors for me to reach even more people. I was amazed to see how God was already redeeming the pain

I had experienced because of losing Jacob. Something I've learned is that in His kingdom, nothing goes to waste. He uses painful seasons, difficult steps of obedience, and even frustrating setbacks to show us His goodness and bring glory to Himself. He can truly do more than we ask or imagine.

When Joshua was preparing to lead the Israelites across the Jordan River into the promised land, he encouraged them with these words: "Consecrate yourselves, for tomorrow the Lord will do amazing things among you" (Josh. 3:5). God had amazing plans for His people in the land of Canaan. He would do miracles there and help them overcome mighty armies. But first they needed to recommit their way to the Lord. They needed to tell Him, "We're all in."

What do you need to surrender to God today? Maybe it's a situation at school or work, or a relationship. Perhaps you've taken on a big challenge and need to trust God with the results. I know from experience that it can be tempting to try to maintain control, but the answer is to just give it to God. Whatever the circumstance, you don't have to know all the details to walk forward in obedience and watch what God will do. You can trust that God will use everything—your pain, your trials, even your missteps—to accomplish His plan. That's such good news, y'all!

When I knelt in my living room that night, surrendering that song to God, I never could have imagined how He would use it. I'm so grateful I trusted my Jesus. I have watched Him do amazing things.

REPEAT AFTER ME:

"I can surrender everything to God and trust Him to use it to accomplish His plan."

Scripture of the Day:

Now to him who is able to do immeasurably more than all we ask or imagine, according to his power that is at work within us, to him be glory in the church and in Christ Jesus throughout all generations, for ever and ever! Amen.

—Ephesians 3:20–21

What is something you need to surrender or "consecrate" to God today?

Think of a time when you trusted God and He did more than you asked for or imagined. How did it increase your trust in His plan and care for you?

Ask the Lord to put someone on your heart with whom you can share your story this week. Listen for His answer and go for it! It might be exactly what they need right now.

Hey, Girl! Let's Talk to God

Write a prayer of surrender telling the Lord you're "all in" and asking Him to deepen your trust in Him.

My Jesus,

In Your powerful name, amen.

DAY 17:

Made New

★ ★ ★

I haven't always understood what it means to be a new creation. When I first gave my life to Jesus, all I knew was that He was real, and I wanted His power in my life. I now know that being a Christian is a lifelong journey of transformation. God doesn't just forgive us; He begins crafting us into the image of His Son. Walking with Him isn't a one-time prayer for salvation; it's waking up every day and saying, "Make me more like You."

I love the words of Ephesians 4:22–24, which say, "You were taught, with regard to your former way of life, to put off your old self… to be made new in the attitude of your minds; and to put on the new self, created to be like God in true righteousness and holiness."

Paul is telling us to *put off* the old self and *put on* the new. It's a two-step process we must repeat over and over throughout our lives. It's not always easy. We all have habits, thought patterns, and ways of dealing with life that cling to us. But when Jesus comes into your heart, He provides the power to change from the inside out.

Before I knew Jesus, I struggled with comparison and worry about the future. After I prayed to receive His salvation, those challenges didn't immediately go away. Change can be uncomfortable, or even painful. At times, I have not wanted to let go of things that used to bring me comfort, such as overeating or impulsive shopping ("retail therapy"). Instead, I gripped tightly to things that felt familiar—even if they weren't good for me—because it felt too hard to change.

Corrie ten Boom, a Dutch Christian who hid Jews during the Holocaust and suffered for four months in a German concentration camp, once said, "I have learned to hold all things loosely, so God will not have to pry them out of my hands."

I've learned that you can't step into who God made you to be while clinging to your old self. Like a torn garment, you must take it off and allow God to dress you in something new. Maybe God's calling you to let go of something to step into a deeper relationship with Him. That can be scary, but it's also exciting. Because every change God leads you through is shaping you to look more like Jesus. Every day is an opportunity to be more like Jesus and reflect His goodness, love, and hope.

We can't claim to be new creations if we're resisting the work God wants to do in us. Are you keeping pace with the ways God is developing you? Are you allowing Him to make your mind new? Are you putting on patience, goodness, and faith? Don't be afraid to leave the familiar behind and go boldly in the direction God is leading. Welcome the changes with joy and anticipation as God shapes your character.

When you begin to see the changes in your life, you'll be amazed. That's the power of Jesus at work in you. You can step forward in confidence, knowing God is transforming you into the woman He created you to be.

REPEAT AFTER ME:

"God is transforming me into the person
He created me to be."

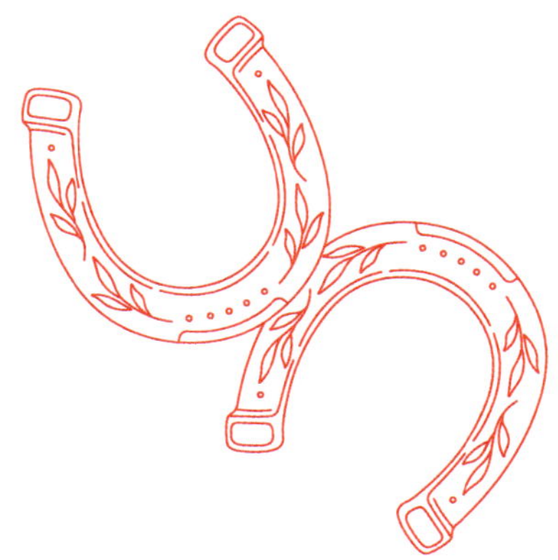

Scripture of the Day:

You were taught, with regard to
your former way of life,
to put off your old self, which
is being corrupted
by its deceitful desires; to be made
new in the attitude of your minds;
and to put on the new self,
created to be like God in true
righteousness and holiness.

—Ephesians 4:22–24

Note to Self

Think about your life: Are you keeping up with the ways God is growing and developing you? What are some changes He might be inviting you into (for example, service opportunities, a daily quiet time with Him, witnessing at school)?

What are some habits, comforts, or attitudes God may be asking you to release for greater growth (for example, excessive screen time, a negative coping mechanism, gossip)?

Ask Him to show you where He is at work in you right now.

Hey, Girl! Let's Talk to God

Write a prayer asking God to help you put off the old self—with its habits, attitudes, and desires—and put on the new self that is being transformed into the image of His Son.

Dear Transforming God,

DAY 18:

A Good Plan

★ ★ ★

I stood in the bathroom at the headquarters of Capitol Christian Music Group as Mom and my sister, Liz, helped me make final adjustments to my appearance. I felt zero nervousness for what lay ahead that day—officially signing with Capitol. Instead I was filled with thankfulness for how the Lord had brought me to this moment.

"I know this is right," I said as they smoothed my hair and adjusted my blouse. "This is exactly where I'm supposed to be. God is going to do something beautiful out of all this—I just know it."

A few minutes later I signed my first music contract, with my family by my side. I knew Jesus was by my side as well.

Later I spoke to the people gathered there. "The Lord has been so faithful to me through all the grief of the past two and a half years," I said. "I'm thankful for this opportunity, and I'm looking forward to what the future holds."

Have you ever had a moment like this, where everything felt right? A moment where you were filled with peace and confidence that you were exactly where you were meant to be? Maybe it came after a chaotic season. Perhaps it happened at an unexpected moment or when you'd felt distant from God. God's Word tells us He leads us in paths of righteousness for His name's sake (Ps. 23:3). When we stay close to Him, even when obedience is difficult, He chooses what is best for us and makes amazing things happen.

That's one of the things I love about Him. You may have heard the verse Jeremiah 29:11, which says, "'For I know the plans I have for you,' declares the LORD, 'plans to prosper you and not to harm you, plans to give you hope and a future.'" He spoke those words to the Israelites, who were going through a hard time of God's judgment. Despite their waywardness and lack of faithfulness to Him, He saw their future. And His plans for them were good.

But notice the next two verses: "Then you will call on me and come and pray to me, and I will listen to you. You will seek me and find me when you seek me with all your heart." This is where we find God's promise. When we pray, He will listen. And when we seek Him with our whole heart, we will find Him.

Choosing a music label was difficult. I was only seventeen years old, and there were several great options. I realized that for me to be successful by my definition—honoring God and telling the world about Him—I would have to listen to *His* voice above all others. I would have to seek *Him* with all my heart. And I would have to follow *Him* alone. When I did, He filled my heart with peace and expectancy. He knew His plans for me, and they were good!

If you have a decision facing you today, stop and pray. Listen for God's voice. Ask Him to lead you. He promises that when you seek Him with all your heart, you will find Him.

REPEAT AFTER ME:

"When I seek God, I will find Him."

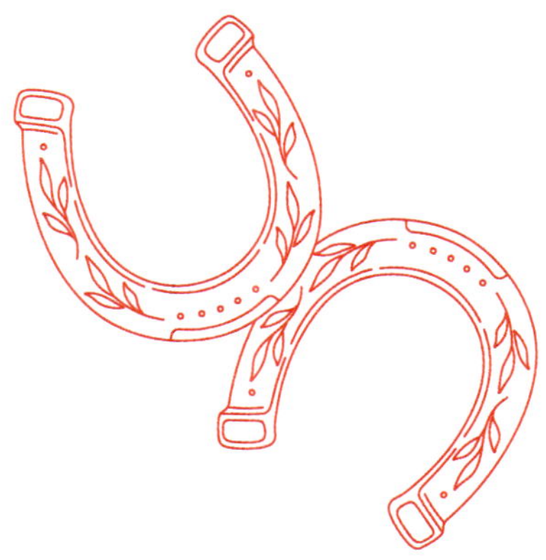

Scripture of the Day:

"For I know the plans I have for you," declares the Lord, "plans to prosper you and not to harm you, plans to give you hope and a future. Then you will call on me and come and pray to me, and I will listen to you. You will seek me and find me when you seek me with all your heart."

—Jeremiah 29:11–13

Note to Self

Think about a tough decision you're currently making or will make in the future. Personalize Jeremiah 29:11–13 in the space provided. (For example, "I know You already know the music label I will sign with and Your plans for me are good. Lead me through Your Word and Your people to the path You have for me.")

What are some ways you can seek God with all your heart? Add to my list!

- Read His Word.
- Pray.
- Worship.
- Consult godly people.
- ______________________________
- ______________________________
- ______________________________

What do you want to trust God with today?

Hey, Girl! Let's Talk to God

Jesus,

You are so good. Thank You for having good plans for my future and leading me on paths of righteousness that fill me with peace. When I have a decision to make, help me to trust You. Thank You for the promise that when I cry out to You, You listen. You don't hide from me, Lord. You are a God who can be found. Help me to listen to Your voice and seek You with my whole heart. I want to be wherever You are and join You in what You are doing.

Amen.

DAY 19:

Christ over the Crash

I still remember the flashing blue lights outside my bedroom window at 3:30 a.m. A few minutes later, six men in uniform stood at our front door. I saw the devastation on my parents' faces and knew something was wrong. My twenty-three-year-old brother, Jacob, had died in a car accident, and our lives were forever changed.

I was only fifteen at the time, and I felt hopeless, like I couldn't take my next breath. But later that night I heard God speak to me: *Anne*, He whispered. *Do you trust Me?*

I responded, "Jesus, I trust You." Immediately I felt a weight lifted off my shoulders. In the middle of heartache, He told me He would give me everything I needed to get through this tragedy. He would give me peace that couldn't be explained. He had a plan for me. From a human standpoint, I would never recover from the blow of losing my beloved big brother. But God… Only He could heal the gaping wound in my heart and bring good from my loss.

When you think about it, God never intended for our lives to be marked by pain and suffering. But when sin entered the world through Adam and Eve, it left us broken. Scripture tells us we will endure trouble and trials in this life that are outside of our control—that's just part of life. But we have a choice: Will we walk alone, trying to figure things out on our own, or will we walk through the valley with Jesus by our side?

I love Jesus' invitation in Matthew 11:28–29: "Come to me, all you who are weary and burdened, and I will give you rest. Take my yoke upon you and learn from me, for I am gentle and humble in heart, and you will find rest for your souls." In our times of deepest need, He offers to carry our burdens and give us rest.

After Jacob died, journaling became a part of my healing process. The outpouring of my heart became songs. One day, as I was flipping through my journal, I noticed that I never wrote just "Jesus" but "My Jesus." *My* Jesus. *Your* Jesus. *Our* Jesus. Adding a pronoun makes all the difference. Through Jesus Christ, the glory of God was cloaked in human flesh. He is not only the Most High God, but He is the One who holds our hearts in our lowest moments. The song "My Jesus" came out of those pages where I desperately called out to Him and watched Him change my life.

While your "crashes" may look different from mine, we all experience trials and tragedy. Your crash may be heartbreaking loss like mine or it may be crushing anxiety or depression. Perhaps it's spiritual doubts or feelings of worthlessness. Regardless of the circumstance, the same Jesus who comforted me can comfort you too. As He makes you new and shapes you to be more like Himself, He also provides His presence, comfort, and life-changing peace.

REPEAT AFTER ME:

"Jesus gives me comfort in hard times."

Scripture of the Day:

Dear friends, do not be surprised at
the fiery ordeal that has come on you
to test you, as though something strange
were happening to you. But rejoice
inasmuch as you participate
in the sufferings of Christ,
so that you may be overjoyed
when his glory is revealed.

—1 Peter 4:12–13

When you think of a difficult "crash" (trial or tragedy) you've experienced, what comes to mind?

Are you willing to let Jesus into your most difficult moments and trust Him today?

What are some ways you've seen Jesus change your life?

Hey, Girl! Let's Talk to God

My Jesus,

You understand all my struggles and invite me to cast my cares on You. Lord, I invite You into all my moments—the painful, difficult ones and the joyful, exhilarating ones. Thank You for offering me Your rest and peace when life doesn't go as I hoped or planned. I may not know my next step, but I know I want to walk with You, my Jesus! Give me the strength I need to endure the hardships I am facing and trust You to use them for good.

Amen.

DAY 20:

Peace in the Pit Stop

★ ★ ★

I'll never forget stopping at a little doughnut shop in Nashville during a family road trip. We were passing through on our way to Florida, like we'd done many times before, but that day was different. As soon as I walked through the door of that shop, I felt a deep sense of peace. Daddy and Jacob had gone in with me, but they didn't seem to notice anything special.

I didn't know what to make of it at the time. I remember thinking, *Why do I feel so content right now?* There was nothing extraordinary about the moment—we were just taking a pit stop on the way to our destination—but God planted something in my heart that day.

A few years later, in January 2018, I walked into the office of the man who would become my first manager. The moment I stepped through the door, the same sense of peace I'd felt in the doughnut shop years earlier washed over me. It felt like God was saying, *I've been working all along, preparing this path and this place for you.*

I didn't have all the answers that day. In fact, I left overwhelmed by the details of what it would take to pursue a music career. What I did have was peace. That peace would carry me through a lot—months of waiting and wondering if this dream God had given me was really going to happen. But every time I found myself back in Nashville, that peace returned.

God's peace is different from what the world offers. It's not the absence of stress or uncertainty; it's God with us in the middle of it. Deuteronomy 31:8 says, "The Lord himself goes before you and will be with you; he will never leave you nor forsake you. Do not be afraid; do not be discouraged." One of the benefits of being made new in Christ is the otherworldly peace He provides to those who follow Him. We don't have to be ruled by worry because God directs our paths.

Sometimes we overlook those "doughnut shop" pit stops where God softly marks a place or a conversation or a person with His peace. But those experiences remind us He's constantly orchestrating the tiniest details of our stories, even when we can't see it.

If you're in a season where you're unsure about what the future holds, ask God to give you His peace. He may not give you a worry-free life or even a feeling that everything's perfect, but He offers something better—a deep assurance that He's with you and He's in control.

When I walked into that doughnut shop, I didn't know that Nashville would be my future home. I had *no idea* all that God had planned for me. But He *did.* And He gave me His peace before I ever needed it. Whatever decisions you may be facing today, listen to the Spirit inside you and let Him give you peace.

REPEAT AFTER ME:

"Whatever decisions I'm facing, God's Spirit gives me peace."

Scripture of the Day:

You will keep
in perfect peace those
whose minds are
steadfast, because
they trust in you.

—Isaiah 26:3

What are some questions or worries you have about your future?

Think of a time when God put you in a place or situation where you felt His peace. What happened?

Hey, Girl! Let's Talk to God

Jesus,

Thank You for Your peace that passes understanding. Thank You for going before me and marking my path with Your presence. Help me to trust You, even when I don't know all the steps ahead. Let me be still long enough to notice Your Spirit. I'll follow wherever You lead.

Amen

SECTION FIVE

You Have Been Saved by Amazing Grace

For it is by grace you have been saved,
through faith—and this is not from yourselves,
it is the gift of God—not by works,
so that no one can boast.

—Ephesians 2:8–9

There's nothing sweeter than knowing your soul is safe in the arms of Jesus. When we say yes to Him and receive His amazing grace, everything changes—not just in eternity but right now, here on earth.

Grace means we don't have to carry the weight of our past anymore. All the shame, the guilt, and the fear are washed away by the blood of Jesus. When you've been saved by grace, your soul finds freedom and rest. Life still gets hard, and you may get weary, but you don't have to face it alone. The King of kings walks with you.

The old hymn says, "Through many dangers, toils and snares / I have already come: / 'tis grace has brought me safe thus far, / and grace will lead me home."[2] That's a truth I've lived. God's grace got me through grief, fear, and heartache—and it'll carry you too.

If you've accepted Jesus, you've received the greatest gift ever given. Walk in confidence, sweet girl. Your soul has been saved by His amazing grace, and no one can take that away.

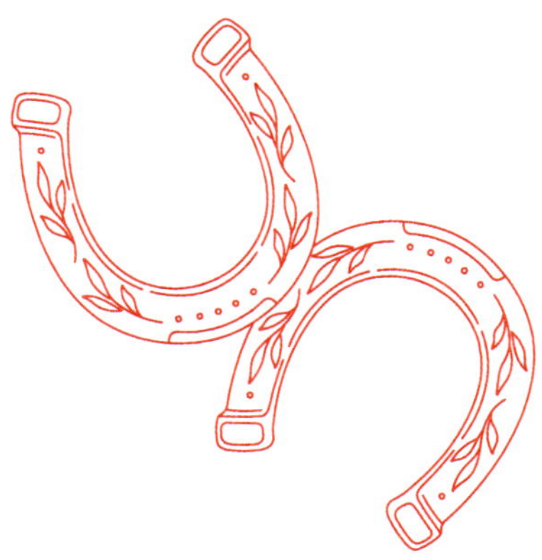

DAY 21:

Seeking God's Presence

★ ★ ★

Have you ever felt abandoned? Maybe you lost someone you loved, or a friend betrayed you. Before Jacob died, I had never felt as forsaken as I did after his loss. I knew God was with me, but some days I felt marooned on an island of pain, stuck and without hope.

In the Gospels we read about Jesus losing a close friend named Lazarus. When Jesus heard His friend was sick, He stayed where He was for two days. His disciples urged Him to go right away, but Jesus reassured them that Lazarus's illness would not end in death (John 11:4). However, Lazarus did die, and by the time Jesus arrived, he had been dead for four days.

I can imagine Jesus sitting with Mary and Martha after He came on the scene. The whole community was devastated and grieving. I wonder if Lazarus was the big brother, little brother, or middle child. Regardless, he was a beloved sibling to Mary and Martha. And he was Jesus' friend.

The shortest verse in the Bible is part of this story. It gives us a glimpse into Jesus' compassionate nature: "Jesus wept" (John 11:35). Even though Jesus knew the rest of the story—that minutes later He would raise Lazarus from the dead—He sat and wept with the grieving sisters.

In my time of feeling alone in my grief, God showed me His deep love and compassion. The psalmist wrote, "Seek the Lord and his strength; seek His presence continually!" (105:4 ESV). When life falls apart and a shadow comes over our souls, Jesus is the One who offers us strength, love, and favor—and a shoulder to cry on. Comfort is found in His presence.

Whatever you are facing today, nothing is too big or too small for Jesus. He is our King, and we are His favored daughters. He wants us to seek Him and allow Him to be a part of everything—good or bad—we're walking through. He sits with us in our pain and sorrow. Even small things, such as hurtful words from a friend or not making the team, matter to Him. He promises to never leave your side or forsake you (Heb. 13:5).

Our world provides ample options of places we can turn for comfort: money, the pleasures of this world, relationships that distract and bring a sense of security. But each of these things passes away, while Jesus provides true comfort through His everlasting love.

Do you feel abandoned today? Are you carrying a burden? Jesus is with you, and He will never fail you. His promises stand firm forever. Whether today is the best day of your life or the worst, Jesus invites you to sit next to Him as He covers you with His love. Seek His presence, and He will give you strength.

REPEAT AFTER ME:

"I can seek God's presence in hard times—He never leaves me."

Scripture of the Day:

You make known
to me the path of life;
you will fill me with joy
in your presence,
with eternal pleasures
at your right hand.

—Psalm 16:11

Note to Self

What do you need from God today (comfort, peace, security, etc.)?

Name one promise from God's Word that is meaningful to you.

List some ways you can seek God's presence today.

Hey, Girl! Let's Talk to God

God of Compassion,

You are sovereign. You know exactly what's going on in my life today. You know whether I feel discouraged or optimistic, worried or at peace. Thank You, Jesus, for understanding my needs today, and inviting me to allow You to meet them. Help me seek Your presence continually and keep my eyes on the things above and not the things of this world. You are the ultimate source of strength, love, and comfort, and all I need is found in You. Thank You for being a compassionate and merciful God.

In Jesus' holy name, amen.

DAY 22:

Beauty from Ashes

★ ★ ★

Have you ever lost someone who was important to you? When Jacob died, I was overwhelmed by grief. In my pain I was tempted to be angry with God for allowing my brother to die. I realized I could fight the grief on my own or move forward with Jesus. The morning after the accident, I sat down at the piano and worship flowed out. I thanked the Lord for my brother and the time I had with him.

Roughly seven hundred years before Jesus was born, the prophet Isaiah spoke these words about the promised Messiah: "He has sent me to bind up the brokenhearted, to proclaim freedom for the captives and release from darkness for the prisoners, to proclaim the year of the LORD's favor and the day of vengeance of our God, to comfort all who mourn, and provide for those who grieve in Zion—to bestow on them a crown of beauty instead of ashes" (Isa. 61:1–3).

When we experience tragedy or trauma, God wants to show us parts of His character that we can't experience any other way than through struggle. When we need healing, we need a Healer. When we need comfort, we need a Comforter. Without our need, we would never understand the depths of God's love and power in our lives.

Jesus does not waste our tragedy or our tears. He draws us close through His comfort and provision. If you are going through a season of suffering, remember that Jesus is with you. He has a plan. Romans 8:28 offers this reminder: "And we know that in all things God works for the good of those who love him, who have been called according to his purpose." Notice that God does not say *all things* are good. He says that in all things *He works* for your good. Whatever your circumstances are, you can be sure God will use it all for His purposes.

God wants the broken pieces of your heart because He cares about every part of you. In Japan they practice an art called *kintsugi*. An artist repairs broken pottery by filling the cracks with gold or silver. The finished work is more beautiful than the original and honors the breaking (and the repair) as a part of the object's history, rather than something to hide. That's how God feels about you. He wants to fill each crack with His love and make your life even more beautiful than before. He is with you in your deepest sorrow. When we are hurt and run into His arms, He scoops us up and holds us close. He cares for our wounds.

When I sat down to worship at the piano, I made the choice to stick with God no matter what. My mom heard me worshiping and asked if I would sing at Jacob's funeral. I agreed, and that was the beginning of God's call on my life to share the good news of the gospel through music. Sometimes purpose waits on the other side of pain. I never could have imagined the good He'd bring out of mine. I know He's with me, and He has created beauty from ashes.

REPEAT AFTER ME:

"Jesus is with me and brings beauty out of my pain."

Scripture of the Day:

And we know that
in all things God works
for the good of those
who love him, who
have been called
according to his purpose.

—Romans 8:28

Note to Self

What does God want to show you about Himself through your current (or past) struggles? Do you need Him as Father, Friend, Comforter, Counselor, Healer, Defender, Provider, Protector, or something else? Ask Him; He wants to show you!

Are there places in your life that feel like ash heaps? Write them down and surrender them to Jesus today.

How can you worship Jesus in the ashes? Add your own ideas to the list I've started:

- Turn on worship music and sing along.
- Take five-minute prayer breaks at home, school, or in the car.
- Turn on the Christian radio station while doing daily tasks.
- Write a prayer of praise to God in your journal.
- Take a walk out in nature and notice the beautiful things He's created.
-
-
-

Hey, Girl! Let's Talk to God

Write a prayer thanking God for working *all things* together for your good.

Dear Healer and Comforter,

Thank You for

You already know the things that feel broken or dead in my life right now. I ask You to

Help me to feel Your presence and peace in this situation:

I surrender my pain to You. Remind me that You are always with me and that You bring beauty out of ashes. Use my story for good. I praise You because

In Jesus' beautiful name, amen.

DAY 23:

Purpose in the Pain

Every time I step onstage, I carry my brother, Jacob, with me.

Telling our story night after night is not easy. In fact, I've learned to talk about my brother without facing the full weight of the loss. But sometimes the pain catches me off guard. I know God has called me to share this testimony. It's not just my story; it's His story of redeeming my pain.

Apart from Jacob's death, I wouldn't be doing what I'm doing. That breaks my heart, but it also gives me purpose. What brings me comfort is that God is with me in everything I do. Every lyric I write, every note I sing, every tear I cry—He sees it all and He's with me. Psalm 34:18 gives us this precious promise: "The Lord is close to the brokenhearted and saves those who are crushed in spirit."

Something amazing happens when pain meets purpose. When I was on the *My Jesus* tour, a little girl told me she had lost her brother too. She had tears streaming down her face. As I wrapped her in a hug, I saw in her a reflection of myself. We were two sisters going through life without our brothers. That moment reminded me why I keep sharing my story.

I was thinking of that little girl, and others like her, when I wrote my song "Rain in the Rearview." The song talks about learning to move forward when your heart still aches. Healing doesn't mean forgetting—I think of Jacob every day and I miss him terribly. But I can put one foot in front of the other because Jesus walks with me.

Maybe you're carrying your own heartache today. I understand, and I wish I could give you a big hug. My message for you is that God will never waste your pain. He sees you. He's holding you close. And He's not finished writing your story. Second Corinthians 1:3–4 says, "Praise be to the God and Father of our Lord Jesus Christ, the Father of compassion and the God of all comfort, who comforts us in all our troubles, so that we can comfort those in any trouble with the comfort we ourselves receive from God." By His grace, God loves to turn our messes into ministry. The sun will shine again. And one day, like me, you'll look back and see that even in the rain, God was leading you forward and giving you a purpose.

REPEAT AFTER ME:

"God gives me purpose in my pain."

Scripture of the Day:

He will wipe every tear from

their eyes. There will be no

more death or mourning

or crying or pain,

for the old order of things

has passed away.

—Revelation 21:4

Note to Self

Heartache shows up in many forms—loss, disappointment, unanswered prayers. What would it look like for you to take a step forward in the middle of painful circumstances?

Think of a situation where God has brought purpose out of your pain. What happened? How did you see God working? How did He bring good from your circumstances?

If you're dealing with loss, don't go it alone. Reach out to someone who cares about you to process your grief. When I lost Jacob, talking to my pastor, mentor, a counselor, and other caring adults helped me cope with the pain and find hope on the other side of loss. You're not alone. Don't be afraid to ask for help.

Hey, Girl! Let's Talk to God

Dear Precious, Heavenly Father,

You know the places in my heart that ache and the memories that still sting. Thank You for Your promise to be close to the brokenhearted and to save the crushed in spirit. Help me to trust You when I don't understand Your plan. Bring purpose out of my pain. Allow my story to encourage someone else who's going through a storm. When I don't feel strong enough to keep going, be my strength. Thank You for never leaving me—even in the rain.

In Your wonderful name, amen.

DAY 24:

Faith on Hard Days

★ ★ ★

There are days when I feel strong and other days when I question whether I'm enough or if I can keep up the pace of writing and recording music, living out of a suitcase, and singing from a different stage every night. Sometimes it feels like my prayers are bouncing off the ceiling, my heart is heavy, and my faith is weak. Maybe you've felt like that too. It can be hard to be a human! (And since Jesus became one, He knows that.)

Here's what I've learned: Faith isn't a feeling—it's a decision. When I was twelve, I decided to make a transition from simply knowing *about* God to having a relationship *with* Him. Just knowing Jesus died and rose again wouldn't change my life; I needed to surrender my life to Him to see real transformation. *Surrender* means giving up control of your life to God, trusting His plan and letting Him be your leader. It's letting Jesus "take the wheel" of your life.

During my first headlining tour, I felt a lot of pressure to perform. I didn't feel fully prepared to be the main singer and entertain and encourage an audience for ninety minutes. One night I stood backstage before a show, feeling completely overwhelmed. On the outside, everything looked perfect—the set and light concept I'd helped to craft, the people cheering, the music from my band beginning to swell. But my emotional state was quite different. I was anxious. I missed my brother. I missed the simplicity of sitting alone with Jesus in my room, worshiping Him away from the spotlight.

I didn't feel strong or up to the task. In that moment I whispered a simple prayer: "Jesus, I don't feel it today. But I believe You're here. Use me for Your glory."

Perseverance doesn't always look like grand gestures or powerful declarations. Sometimes it looks like showing up when you'd rather stay home or singing when you're still grieving. It looks like spending time reading God's Word and praising Him when your heart feels numb. It's choosing to keep walking—one foot in front of the other—because you know who walks beside you.

In Hebrews the author reminds us: "Now faith is confidence in what we hope for and assurance about what we do not see" (11:1). We can stand firm in what we know to be true even when our emotions tell a different story. You don't have to *feel* strong to keep going. Keep talking to Jesus. Keep trusting that He's working beyond what you can see. Jesus said that faith as small as a mustard seek is powerful enough to move mountains.

If your heart feels discouraged today or your prayers feel weak, choose faith and perseverance. Walk forward, even if it's small steps. Say a short prayer. Listen to a worship song. Read a psalm. And remember, Jesus is with you.

★ ★ ★

REPEAT AFTER ME:

"I can choose faith when I feel weak or tired."

Scripture of the Day:

Now faith is
confidence in what
we hope for
and assurance
about what we
do not see.

—Hebrews 11:1

Note to Self

What practices strengthen your faith on hard days?

Read 2 Corinthians 12:10. How do Paul's words encourage you?

Hey, Girl! Let's Talk to God

Dear Gracious and Heavenly Father,

Lord, some days I feel so weak and inadequate. Help me hold on to faith when my eyes can't see what You're doing. I praise You for Your promises and the ways You're constantly working behind the scenes to fulfill Your purposes. Help me believe You are working, You are with me, and You have a plan. Thank You for being a faithful God in all seasons.

In Your holy name, amen.

DAY 25:

Carrying Jesus into the World

★ ★ ★

When I crossed into country music with the *Rebel* album, I experienced a sense of whiplash. One day, I was leading my first headlining Christian tour with the *My Jesus* album, and the next, I was stepping onto a country music stage for the first time ever. Two different worlds but the same message: Jesus saves.

It was wild—I felt everything from excitement to straight-up fear. I remember calling my manager before my first country music tour as an opener for Scotty McCreery and saying, "What if they boo me off the stage?" It's easy to share Jesus when you're in a church or singing to a room full of believers, but stepping into a space where people might not be expecting to hear about faith required a new level of courage.

Something I've thought about is that Jesus didn't stay in safe spaces. He didn't only hang out with religious folks. He went to the poor, the sick, and those in need of healing and forgiveness. He ate with sinners. He walked dusty roads, welcomed children, and sat in fishing boats to preach to ordinary crowds of men and women. He didn't wait for people to come to Him—He went to them.

And He calls us to do the same. Jesus told His disciples to "go into all the world and preach the gospel to all creation" (Mark 16:15). I grew up hearing that verse in church, but as God provides new opportunities—and new stages—I've really taken it to heart.

The first time I stood onstage during my country music tour, I didn't know how it would go. People came to have fun—not necessarily to hear about Jesus. Watching God move blew my mind and strengthened my faith. I had people tell me that they gave their lives to Christ at one of those concerts! Jesus can meet people anywhere, y'all. It doesn't have to be in a church. It may be at your track meet, while you're doing 4-H at the fair, or as you're serving up lattes at your job.

Following Jesus is about having boldness to step out of my comfort zone, even when it's scary. I've learned it's not that difficult when I walk in the footsteps of the One who came to seek and to save.

If you feel that tug to take your faith outside the four walls of the church, let me be the first to say—do it! Take the message of hope God's given you to people who desperately need to hear the good news. Tell your story of faith even if your voice shakes. Tell them how your soul's been saved by His amazing grace. You never know, someone might meet Jesus because of your courage.

REPEAT AFTER ME:

"I can take God's message of hope to those who need it."

Scripture of the Day:

Have I not commanded you? Be strong and courageous. Do not be afraid; do not be discouraged, for the Lord your God will be with you wherever you go.

—Joshua 1:9

Note to Self

Make a list of (unexpected) places where you could share Jesus:

★

★

★

★

★

One easy way to talk about Jesus is by sharing your faith story, often called a "testimony." Here are a few questions to help you formulate your testimony:

When did you first meet Jesus?

Who told you about Him?

Write about when you asked Jesus into your life and decided to follow Him.

How has Jesus made a difference in your life and helped you through challenging times?

Why would you tell someone else they should follow Jesus?

Hey, Girl! Let's Talk to God

Strong and Mighty God,

Thank You for giving me a story to share. I pray You would give me boldness to speak Your name in places where it's not always comfortable. Help me to be strong and courageous in sharing Your truth. Remind me that You go before me, and You meet people right where they are. Help me be a light in the darkness and a rebel for Your kingdom. My desire is to follow You, even when it's uncomfortable. Use me, Lord, in all spaces and places You send me.

Amen.

SECTION SIX

Glad We Had This Talk

Therefore encourage one another
and build each other up,
just as in fact you are doing.

—1 Thessalonians 5:11

God didn't design us to walk through life alone. He gave us community—real Christ-centered friendships—to remind us we belong, we're loved, and we're stronger together. That's what the body of Christ—the church—is all about. We're here to lift one another up when life gets hard, celebrate each other's victories, and keep pointing one another to Jesus.

Some days, we're the ones who need the encouragement. Other days, we get to be the encourager. Both are beautiful parts of God's plan. I've learned that true friendship isn't just about having fun, though that's part of it. Friendship is about having each other's back. It's about standing in faith together, praying for one another, and showing up when life feels heavy. That's real love.

If you've got people in your life who speak truth, remind you of who you are in Christ, and walk with you through the valleys—thank God for them today. And be that kind of friend for someone else. We're better when we build each other up.

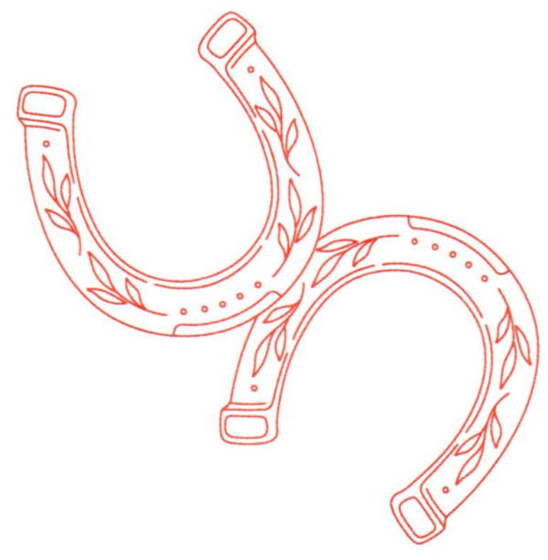

DAY 26:

The Best Kind of Friend

★ ★ ★

When I was in junior high, some girls I thought were my friends turned on me. I found out they had been saying mean things behind my back—and it absolutely crushed me. I remember walking through those days feeling so hurt, confused, and alone. It's hard to put into words the pain that comes when people you trust let you down.

I really connected with that line in my song "Hey Girl" about everybody and their mother telling me what I was worth. The drama of mean girls became overwhelming, and I felt as if the situation would never get better. If you've been in a situation where other girls were mean to you, I wish I could give you a big hug. You are so precious to God, and it hurts His heart when people are cruel or unkind to one of His daughters. Navigating cliques, mean girls, and gossip can feel like a trial that won't end. (But it does—hang in there, sweet girl!)

In the middle of my heartbreak, God gave me one faithful friend. A friend who loved Jesus and reminded me that no matter what people said or did, I was deeply loved by God. I'll never forget how powerful it was to have someone speak truth to me when I felt so broken. It taught me something I carry with me today—the people we allow to be close to us matter more than we realize.

Proverbs 18:24 (ESV) says, "A man of many companions may come to ruin, but there is a friend who sticks closer than a brother." This verse reminds us that while we may have many acquaintances, we should be on the lookout for loyal, trustworthy friends who don't leave when the going gets tough.

Some people don't have our best interests at heart and would happily lead us to activities or choices God says will hurt us. It's important to be discerning about who we allow in our lives. When Paul wrote to the Corinthians, he said, "Do not be misled: 'Bad company corrupts good character'" (1 Cor. 15:33). The people we spend the most time with shape who we become. Our closest friends should be those who share our convictions and push us closer to Christ.

Jesus Himself chose a group of close friends. He had twelve disciples, but within that group, He shared a deeper connection with Peter, James, and John. Those three were with Him in the hardest and holiest moments. Jesus poured into them. And still, even Jesus experienced betrayal from someone in His circle—Judas. If you've been betrayed or hurt, Jesus understands completely.

What amazes me most is that the King of kings calls us friends!

In John 15:15 He says, "I no longer call you servants.... Instead, I have called you friends." That means you're not just tolerated by Jesus—you're treasured.

If you're in a lonely season, you're not alone. Jesus is your truest friend. You can talk to Him, cry with Him, and lean on Him. That's what I did in lonely seasons where friends were hard to come by. And if you're praying for godly friends, don't give up. Ask God to bring people into your life who love Him and will be loyal friends.

You were created for connection. And Jesus will never leave your side—even when others do.

REPEAT AFTER ME:

"Jesus is my best friend and helps me choose the right kind of companions."

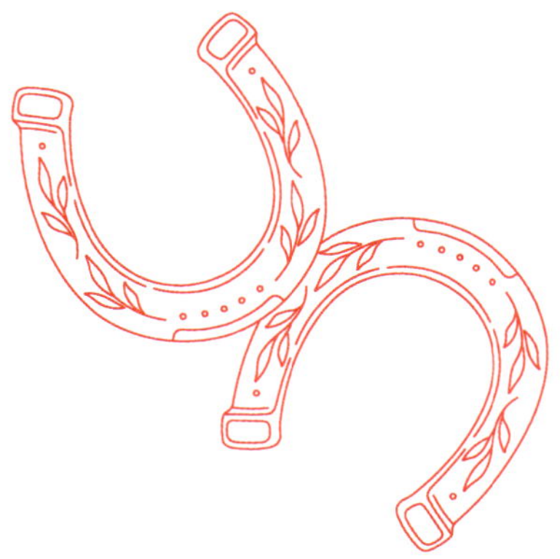

Scripture of the Day:

A man of many companions may come to ruin, but there is a friend who sticks closer than a brother.

—Proverbs 18:24 ESV

Note to Self

What qualities do you look for in a friend?

1.

2.

3.

Who is in your inner circle?

How can you be the kind of friend described in Proverbs 18:24?

Hey, Girl! Let's Talk to God

Lord,

Thank You for calling me Your friend and never leaving my side. Help me choose friends who push me closer to You and help me stand strong in my faith. Help me to be wise in choosing my friends and give me the courage to walk away from relationships that pull me away from You. Heal the wounds in my heart from past betrayals and bring godly people into my life who will love me like You do. Show me how to be loyal, trustworthy, encouraging, and loving to the friends You've put in my life. I pray we would build one another up and inspire one another to be women of courage and character.

In Your precious name, amen.

DAY 27:

Better Together

★ ★ ★

Have you ever worked together with a group to accomplish a goal? Maybe you've served on a mission trip, played on a sports team, or been part of a school play. There's something so special about linking arms with others to do something meaningful. It fills your heart and reminds you that we weren't created to do life alone.

I got to experience this when I started writing songs for my *Rebel* album. I started writing when I was out on my very first headlining tour. I remember sitting on the bus, scratching down ideas in my journal, and dreaming about my next album, which I hoped would mix the heart of Christian music with the twang of country.

When I got back to Nashville, I teamed up with some incredible writers, including a few new friends from the country music world. We went off to what we called "writing camps"—where we'd spend days together laughing, praying, and pouring our hearts into songwriting. There was a whiteboard covered in titles and lyrics, coffee mugs everywhere, and this contagious creative energy that can only come from the Holy Spirit.

I loved every second of it.

Those days weren't just about making music; they were about connection. We shared stories, opened up about our struggles, and leaned on each other for ideas and encouragement. I remember thinking, *This is what the body of Christ is supposed to feel like. Different people bringing their gifts, blending them together for something greater than ourselves.*

Paul talked about this exact thing in 1 Corinthians 12:18–21: "God has placed the parts in the body, every one of them, just as he wanted them to be. If they were all one part, where would the body be? As it is, there are many parts, but one body. The eye cannot say to the hand, 'I don't need you!' And the head cannot say to the feet, 'I don't need you!'"

We need one another, y'all! I never would have been able to write sixteen songs by myself. (Well, I could have tried, but they wouldn't have been as good!) Each writer brought something different to the table through his or her life experiences, musical influences, creativity, and talent. When I sing these songs now, I hear those friends in every note.

That's the beauty of the body of Christ. We each bring something unique, and when we put them all together, the gospel shines brighter. Maybe you're like a nose—serving an obvious function, there for all to see. Or maybe you're a pinky toe, tucked away but providing critical balance to the body. God has placed the parts of the body exactly as He wants them, so that together they can spread the good news and build His kingdom.

If you're already surrounded by strong teammates, take a moment to thank God for them. What a blessing! Treasure those relationships and cheer one another on. If you're not in a community, look for some people to link arms with. Following Jesus is way better when we do it together.

REPEAT AFTER ME:

"God gives me community to help me accomplish good works."

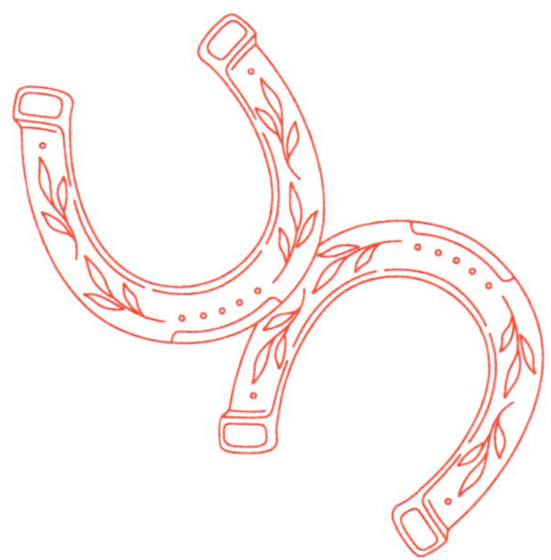

Scripture of the Day

Let us consider
how we may spur one another
on toward love and good
deeds, not giving up meeting
together, as some are
in the habit of doing,
but encouraging
one another—and all
the more as you see
the Day approaching.

—Hebrews 10:24–25

Note to Self

What body part in the body of Christ do you imagine yourself to be? Draw a picture and list a few of your best functions. (For example, draw a picture of a hand and write, "I'm a helping hand because I love to help people and be of service.")

Think of a time when you worked with other Christians toward a common goal. What happened? How did it make you feel?

What are two ways you can contribute to the body of believers?

1.

2.

Hey, Girl! Let's Talk to God

Loving Father,

Thank You for creating us to need one another. I praise You for Your wisdom in arranging the parts of the body to work together in harmony and build up Your kingdom. Thank You for making us each different and giving us a variety of gifts and abilities to love and serve one another. Thank You for the people You've put in my life to encourage, help, and support me—family, friends, mentors, and teachers. Thank You for the beautiful gift of community and connection. Help me contribute to the body of believers for Your glory, Jesus.

Amen.

DAY 28:

Sunday Sermons

★ ★ ★

I grew up going to church, a fact that I'm both proud of and grateful for. I remember sitting with my family in the third row every Sunday, listening to the preacher and examining the red letters in my Bible that held Jesus' words for me. I didn't fully understand it all back then, and I hadn't yet made a personal decision to follow Jesus, but those moments planted seeds of truth in my heart. They built a foundation I still stand on today. (I wrote about it in my song "Sunday Sermons.")

Thanks to those early experiences in church, I had a rich understanding of God's Word from a young age. I also had an extended family of believers—people who encouraged me, prayed for me, and showed me what it looked like to walk with Jesus. As a teenager, I realized all I had learned about God was true and encountered Him as a person who wanted to have a relationship with me. That's when a true transformation of my life began.

Not everyone shares my story. In fact, today many young people are walking away from the church altogether. I hear people say they believe in God but not religion, or that they're spiritual but not interested in organized worship. Some are just plain busy and feel like church doesn't fit into their schedule. The truth we must realize is that this drift away from church isn't harmless; it's a tactic of the enemy.

The church isn't just a building or something to do on Sunday morning. It's the body of Christ—the people of God coming together to worship, grow, and be equipped to go back out and be a light. When we stop showing up, we miss out on the blessings God has for us. Here are just a few truths Scripture gives us about the church:

- ★ The gates of hell shall not prevail against it (Matt. 16:18).
- ★ Jesus obtained it with His own blood (Acts 20:28).
- ★ It is a place to stir one another up to love and good works (Heb. 10:24).
- ★ It was built as a dwelling place for God, through the Spirit (Eph. 2:22).
- ★ Christ is its head, and the church is His bride (Eph. 5:25).

Our world may be drifting away from the pews, but the church is still God's plan A. It's where we get encouraged. Church is the place where we encourage one another, use our spiritual gifts, and receive power to do God's work. I'm so thankful for godly pastors who preached truth, worship leaders who led with passion, and the community of believers that helped grow my faith. God used the church to reach me—and He continues to use it to reach people today.

Are you connected to a local church? If not, what's holding you back? Maybe you've been hurt by church before or you're just out of the habit. Maybe you're nervous to go alone. I understand, but I want to encourage you: Don't let the enemy convince you that isolation is the easier path. You were made for community. You were made to be part of the body.

Make a plan to attend. Ask a friend to go with you, and pray for God to lead you to the right church family. Because when you plug into a place where God's Word is preached and His presence is honored, you'll grow, and your life will change.

REPEAT AFTER ME:

"God gives me church to experience community and mature my faith."

Scripture of the Day

His intent was that now, through the church, the manifold wisdom of God should be made known to the rulers and authorities in the heavenly realms, according to his eternal purpose that he accomplished in Christ Jesus our Lord.

—Ephesians 3:10–11

What positive experiences have you had with church?

Are you plugged into a local church? Sunday morning attendance is a great start, but what step can you take to go deeper? (Examples: join a Bible study or small group, volunteer to serve, attend youth group, etc.)

How might God use you in your church to encourage others and stir them to love and good works?

Hey, Girl! Let's Talk to God

Jesus,

Thank You for establishing Your church to accomplish Your work on earth. Help me honor You as I attend church and serve You through a local body of believers. I pray You would teach me Your truth and help me to encourage others to do the things You're calling them to. I pray for wisdom and spiritual protection for my pastor. Lord, give the people in my church love and unity so that we may win many to Christ.

In Your holy name I pray, Jesus, amen.

DAY 29:

True Connection

When I moved to live in Nashville full-time in 2021, I felt like I'd been pulled away from the only home I'd ever known. I missed my family and friends back in Lexington. Not only was I in a different state from everyone I loved, but I was also living a different lifestyle than my friends back home. I wasn't attending college classes or hanging out with people on the weekend like other nineteen-year-olds. I was traveling the country, giving concerts, and telling my story to thousands of strangers. I loved what I was doing, but I was also lonely.

We live in a world where it's easy to feel connected but not be truly known. Social media, instant messaging, and even our favorite TV shows or podcasts give us a false sense of closeness with others. But in a quiet evening at home, when your phone doesn't light up, it can feel like everyone else has a circle, or a person, except for you. I've felt that.

Even on tour, when I'm meeting hundreds of people in a night and I'm surrounded by my tour family (and actual family!), I've had moments of feeling unseen. It's wild how you can be surrounded by people and still feel alone. The good news is that God sees us, and He understands. In the beginning God declared, "It is not good for the man to be alone" (Gen. 2:18). We were created for authentic, iron-sharpens-iron friendships. We need people in our lives who speak truth in love, remind us of who we are in Christ, and help us shoulder life's burdens.

Over the past few years, God has blessed me with some precious soul-deep friends. I know I can reach out to them anytime and they will drop everything to help me out. And I'd do the same for them. The thing is—real friendships require effort. It's easier to stay home binge-watching your favorite show than set up a coffee date or take a walk with someone. But when we press in to form deeper connections, God uses those relationships to produce peace and joy in our lives.

If you're feeling lonely today, I see you. More importantly, Jesus sees you. He knows our hearts crave connection, and He can help us grow in our friendships. Lonely seasons will come, but Jesus, the greatest friend of all, is there to help us find and nurture strong friendships.

REPEAT AFTER ME:

"Jesus can help me grow in my friendships."

Scripture of the Day

Two are better than one,
because they have a good
return for their labor:
If either of them falls down,
one can help the other up.
But pity anyone who
falls and has no one to
help them up.

—Ecclesiastes 4:9–10

Note to Self

Take a friend inventory. List your closest friends and something each contributes to your life.

Ex. Laney → encourages me and always points me to Jesus!

→

→

→

Think of a few people God might be prompting you to reach out to. Who needs encouragement, or even just someone to sit with them? List a few potential new friends and a plan to connect.

Ex. Ava (from Bible study) → Ask her to get coffee this week.

→

→

→

Hey, Girl! Let's Talk to God

Jesus,

Thank You for being a friend who never leaves. You know how my heart craves connection and how I long for someone to laugh with, pray with, and do life with. Lord, please bring the right kind of friends into my life who will push me closer to You. Help me to care for my friends with Your love. Show me people I can reach out to. In my lonely moments, help me to remember that You are enough. Teach me to be a friend like You are—faithful, kind, and full of grace.

In Your name, amen.

DAY 30:

A Guide in the Wilderness

★ ★ ★

"So, what is God saying to *you*, Anne?"

My mentor, Erica, asked the question I'd been expecting. I was at a crossroads in my life and felt uncertain about what decision to make. Should I start looking into colleges, go to worship school, to hone my musical skills for a career as a church worship leader, or pursue a music career in Nashville? All I knew was I wanted to be in a place where I could grow in the Lord and use my gifts for His kingdom.

Erica gently reminded me that God would give me the godly desires of my heart, and that I could trust my parents' advice as I waited on what the Lord had planned. I took Erica's words to heart, and a few months later—in His perfect timing—God provided the money needed for me to pursue a music career.

That season felt like trekking through the wilderness. I knew God was with me, but I couldn't see what He was doing or how He was providing. I recently heard someone say: "When you're in the wilderness, you need an experienced guide." Erica has been one of those guides for me. When I'm facing a tough decision or going through a challenging time, I know I can count on her wise, truth-filled counsel and prayers.

Second Timothy offers an example of mentorship when Paul encouraged the young pastor Timothy: "The things you have heard me say in the presence of many witnesses entrust to reliable people who will also be qualified to teach others" (2:2). Paul trained Timothy in faith and godliness so he could do the same for others. In a similar passage in Titus, Paul encouraged older women to train younger women in biblical truth and the everyday work of following Jesus.

Mentors point you to the truth and cheer you on through life's challenges. You can turn to them when you need direction, encouragement, or prayer. Do you have a mentor in your life? If not, ask God to show you someone who can walk with you—someone who can pray with you and speak wisdom into your story.

And if you're further down the road in your faith, maybe He's calling you to do that for someone else. No matter what the wilderness looks like, God always makes a way. And often, that way comes through faithful, Spirit-filled guides like Erica, who point us to truth and help us hold on to hope.

REPEAT AFTER ME:

"I need mentors and guides to help me on my journey of faith."

Scripture of the Day

Walk with the wise and become wise, for a companion of fools suffers harm.

—Proverbs 13:20

Have you ever walked through a "wilderness season"? What helped you come out of it?

Do you have a spiritual mentor—a person of faith with whom you speak regularly? How has this person helped you in your spiritual journey?

Who is someone you might be able to mentor?

Hey, Girl! Let's Talk to God

All-Knowing God,

Sometimes I feel like I'm wandering in the wilderness, needing to hear from You. Lord, please provide experienced guides to point me to Your truth and encourage me when I'm in those seemingly dry and barren places. I know You're always working and You are a waymaker. Help me to pass along to others the truth and wisdom I receive from those who invest in me. As I walk with others who love and honor You, make me wise.

In Your name I pray, amen.

SECTION SEVEN

A Little Last Advice

If any of you lacks wisdom, you should ask God, who gives generously to all without finding fault, and it will be given to you.

—James 1:5

The Christian life isn't always mountaintops and sunshine. Sometimes it's valleys and storm clouds. I've walked through seasons where I've felt full of purpose, peace, and joy. But I've also had seasons where I've battled doubt, insecurity, and paralyzing fear. Life is hard sometimes, and we all need Jesus to get through it!

One thing I've come to know is this: God is my Rock when I feel unsteady. He hears my prayers, provides people to encourage me, and leads me on straight paths. Whether it's the conversations I'm having, the relationships I'm building, the resources I'm stewarding, or the decisions I'm making, He is just a prayer away when I need direction. The Holy Spirit convicts and guides me, giving me confidence to choose the right path.

Whether we're facing important decisions or walking through hardship, we can always ask God for wisdom. He tells us He'll give it generously. Keep trusting Him through every decision. Keep your heart soft and your eyes fixed on Jesus. He promises to give you everything you need.

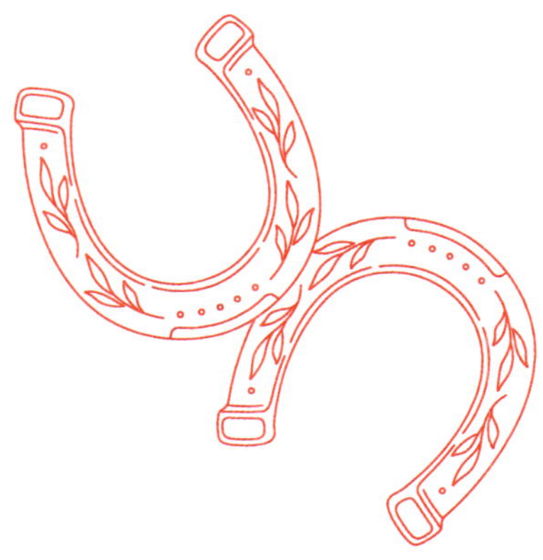

DAY 31:

Speak Life

★ ★ ★

Words hold power. They can build up or tear down, bless or bruise. And if we're not careful, we can find ourselves speaking death over the very things God wants to breathe life into.

When I was a teenager, I struggled with people saying unkind, untrue things about me. I was devastated and wanted to fight back. But when I talked to my mom, she said, "Kill them with kindness, Anne. You don't know what they're going through. They have their own pain and insecurities motivating them to say those things. Pray for them."

In the moment, I wasn't crazy about her advice, but I've never forgotten it. Her approach echoes Proverbs 18:21, which says, "The tongue has the power of life and death."

Our words are more powerful than we know. Our words can lead someone closer to Jesus or push them away from Him. Although it might feel good in the moment to unleash a few choice words on someone who's wronged me, as a follower of Jesus, I'm called to respond in love.

James 3:5–6 reminds us that our words can be like a spark that lights a wildfire: "The tongue is a small part of the body, but it makes great boasts. Consider what a great forest is set on fire by a small spark. The tongue also is a fire, a world of evil among the parts of the body. It corrupts the whole body, sets the whole course of one's life on fire, and is itself set on fire by hell."

That's a pretty serious warning about the destructive power of words. I've seen this in my own life. There have been times I've said things out of emotion—hurt, fear, even pride—and before I knew it, that one word became a flame that hurt someone's feelings or damaged a relationship. Once words are spoken, you can't take them back. You can apologize and receive forgiveness, but hurtful words can't be unsaid…or unheard.

Jesus always spoke life through His words. He called people out of darkness, shame, and fear. Though His words were powerful, people were drawn to His compassion. When I speak words of life, I reflect God's love. What does it look like to speak life?

★ It's pausing when someone upsets me—so I can offer a kind response.

★ It's speaking words of encouragement when I see God working in someone's life.

★ It's thanking (blessing) those who care for me.

★ It's choosing to speak the truth in love to someone I care about.

★ It's listening before I speak and offering a gentle answer.

As a music artist, I speak (and sing) many words every day. I speak from stage at my concerts, I visit with fans, and I have conversations with my family members, people I work with, and close friends. Every conversation is an opportunity for me to bring life or bring death—to help or to hurt. Even the smallest word, spoken in love, can revive a weary heart. Let's speak life to others and watch the difference it makes.

REPEAT AFTER ME:

"God helps me speak words that bring life."

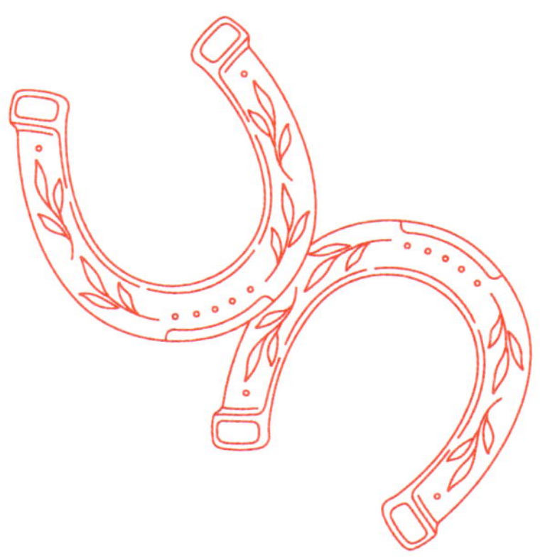

Scripture of the Day

Do not let any unwholesome talk come out of your mouths, but only what is helpful for building others up according to their needs, that it may benefit those who listen.

—Ephesians 4:29

Note to Self

Think about the conversations you have during a typical day. Are the words you speak life-giving? Make a list of types of speech that bring life, such as "words of encouragement" or "a gentle response."

Write down some words that someone spoke to you—or you spoke to someone—that were life-giving.

Reflect on trouble areas you have when it comes to your words (gossip, bickering, harsh words, etc.). Write them down and ask God to put out those sparks and guard your mouth from destructive words.

Pray and ask God to forgive you for speaking words that tear down and ask Him for wisdom to make things right.

Ask God to help you speak life-giving words that build up others.

Hey, Girl! Let's Talk to God

Gracious Lord,

Thank You for the gift of words. You have created our words to be so powerful, Jesus. They can crush or cure. Help me to be a woman who speaks words that encourage, inspire, and bring hope. I ask for self-control to avoid speaking words that tear down or bring death. May my speech always be gracious and reflect Your truth and love. Lord, use me to speak life into a world that so badly needs it.

In Your precious name, amen.

DAY 32:

Walking Away from Red Flags

★ ★ ★

Hey, girl! Let's talk about romantic relationships for a minute. Relationships can be one of life's greatest blessings—and one of its biggest challenges. Romantic feelings are big and exciting and can cloud our judgment. When we're swept up in the emotions of love or attraction, it's easy to ignore the quiet tug of the Holy Spirit, signaling something's not right. We may want to believe the best and see the potential in the person we like, but God is throwing up some major red flags.

In my song "Red Flag" I talked about some of the things I'm looking for in a man. Above all, he has to love Jesus more than me. He needs to attend church and be growing in his faith. And I'm looking for someone down to earth, who respects me and isn't afraid of hard work. Some of my preferences are that he loves the outdoors as much as I do and enjoys hunting and fishing.

What traits do you hope for in a future partner? It's great to write down a list of nonnegotiable qualities. That makes it easy to discern when a potential relationship isn't looking promising. But sometimes we're excited about a relationship, and we ignore the warning signs. We convince ourselves that we should extend grace or give them the benefit of the doubt.

Another way to make wise decisions in relationships is to seek the advice of strong Christians in your life. Talk with someone you trust, someone who can evaluate the relationship with a clear perspective, and give that person permission to speak into your life. When your judgment is clouded by infatuation, parents, mentors, and trusted friends can help you see more clearly. And when they warn you, listen! Don't defend or fight. Take their advice to heart because you already decided they are trustworthy and love you enough to tell you the truth. God might just be speaking through them to protect you.

Maybe you've been in a relationship with someone who wasn't sold out for Jesus. You may have tried talking yourself into it by focusing on the person's good qualities. But the fact was, you weren't walking the same road. This is the reason the Bible instructs us to be joined only with believers and not to be "unequally yoked" (2 Cor. 6:14 ESV). That concept comes from the agricultural practice of teaming up two oxen to pull equally and work efficiently together. God knows it's best for you to be joined with a man who shares your faith and values. Together you can be a powerful team!

The Bible also talks about red flags. Proverbs 27:12 says, "The prudent see danger and take refuge, but the simple keep going and pay the penalty." It's wisdom, not weakness, to walk away from danger. It's obedience, not quitting, to set boundaries. You can trust that God sees what you can't, such as the future and the condition of a person's heart. When He shows you a red flag—whether it's dishonesty, manipulation, disrespect, or spiritual immaturity—take it to heart.

God doesn't withhold good things from us (Ps. 84:11). When He tells us *no* or *not yet*, it's because He has something, or *someone*, better. Maybe He's wanting to do something deeper in your heart before you team up with another person. Perhaps He's teaching you how to find your identity in Him alone or shaping you to be the kind of partner your future spouse needs. The Bible tells us to trust in the Lord in all areas of life, and that includes romantic relationships.

Ladies, don't settle for someone who only halfway loves Jesus. Look for someone who honors God, listens to truth, and encourages your calling. And if red flags pop up? Pay attention. Ask God for the strength to walk away when something feels off or you know a relationship isn't His best for you. The Holy Spirit is your guide, and He speaks through Scripture, wise counselors, and an abiding sense of peace.

If you've made relationship mistakes in the past, God offers you a fresh start. Confess your sin to Him, and He will cleanse you from all unrighteousness (1 John 1:9). Never forget that you are a priceless treasure of the God who loves you! Your worth isn't up for debate. God will bring the right person at the right time—and until then, He's shaping you into the woman He created you to be.

★ ★ ★

REPEAT AFTER ME:

"God can help me have wisdom in romantic relationships."

Scripture of the Day

The prudent see danger
and take refuge,
but the simple
keep going and
pay the penalty.

—Proverbs 27:12

Note to Self

Have you ever ignored a red flag in a relationship? What happened?

What qualities do you want in a godly partner? Are you becoming that kind of person yourself?

Are you trusting God with your love life or trying to control it? What step can you take this week to surrender this area of your life to God?

Say a prayer surrendering your love life to God. Ask Him to open and shut the doors He chooses. Every time you develop feelings for someone, surrender those emotions to God, seek Him (and ask for wisdom!), and trust Him with the outcome.

Hey, Girl! Let's Talk to God

Loving Father,

Thank You that I can trust You in every area of life, including my love life. You know the desires of my heart, and I believe You don't withhold good things from Your children. I pray that You would open my eyes to red flags. Help me not to fear letting go or stepping out of a bad relationship when You're calling me into something better. Help me to honor You with my mind, soul, and body. I trust You have good plans for me and that You are doing a deep work in my heart as I trust in You. Help me to surrender my relationships to You, Jesus, and wait for Your best for my life.

Amen.

DAY 33:

Words That Heal

★ ★ ★

There's something about old trees that takes my breath away. I love the ones with wide, winding branches and roots that run deep into the soil. Strong and steady, they've weathered storms and seasons and are still standing.

As a child, my favorite tree was a large willow in our backyard. My siblings and I called it "the jumping tree" because it was so tall, you literally had to jump into it! As kids, Jacob, Elizabeth, and I would help each other scramble up that giant tree until we found our perfect spots. We spent many happy hours in its shaded branches—sharing secrets, stories, and jokes. We bonded and provided each other with love, joy, and comfort.

That's the picture Proverbs 15:4 gives us of comforting words: "The soothing tongue is a tree of life, but a perverse tongue crushes the spirit."

This image is beautiful, but also sobering. Our words carry weight. I've been crushed by a careless comment, and I've been lifted by a few words spoken at the right time. Words have the power to be a tree that brings life—covering others with peace and inspiring hope—or like a wet blanket that crushes someone's spirit.

One of the reasons words are so important to me is because God has given me a ministry of using them through my songs and encouraging people from the stage. That's why Hey Girl Nation is so precious to me. I've discovered that life-giving words come from hearts rooted in Jesus. When we're filled up with His love and truth, that comes out in what we say. I think of all those sweet conversations I had with my siblings in that willow tree. I felt treasured and knew I belonged. I want to soothe hearts and build confidence the way Jacob and Elizabeth did for me.

Think about someone who needs your life-giving words today—a teacher, a grandparent, your pastor. A well-timed word of kindness can make a big difference in someone's life. Maybe you have a friend going through a hard time or your brother or sister needs some extra encouragement. Maybe your mom needs to hear, "Thank you for all you do. I notice." Ask God to help you speak words that comfort instead of crush.

And don't forget about *you*! When you feel anxious or weary, speak truth over yourself. Repeat after me: "I'm a blood-bought, battle-fought daughter of the King. I am a new creation in Christ. The Holy Spirit gives me the power to follow Jesus and say no to sin. He will never leave me. I am held in His loving arms. He is in control." Speak these truths when you need peace. God speaks words of life over you and helps you comfort others through what you say.

REPEAT AFTER ME:

"I can speak words that comfort and don't crush."

Scripture of the Day

Gracious words are a honeycomb, sweet to the soul and healing to the bones.

—Proverbs 16:24

Note to Self

Who would you like to bless with comforting words? On the notes below write what you could say to each person. It could be a Bible verse, an encouragement, or a simple reminder of truth ("God loves you, and so do I").

Hey, Girl! Let's Talk to God

Jesus,

Let my words bring life to those around me. Teach me to speak words of love, truth, and peace. Keep my heart in tune with Yours so what I say reflects Your character and heart. Use my voice to bring comfort to the people around me and give them hope. Make me like that tree—strong, steady, and full of grace, inviting others into a place where they feel seen and known.

In Your precious name, amen.

DAY 34:

Truth in Times of Transition

★ ★ ★

Moving to Nashville at nineteen and taking on a life of writing, recording, and touring was exhilarating but also challenging. I had to find my way in a new community and navigate the long hours and sleep deprivation of being a touring music artist. A planner by nature, I found that all the unknowns were tough for me. Stepping through the doors God was opening in rapid succession required a new level of trust and courage. I didn't always feel up to the task.

Thankfully I had people in my life who encouraged me that God had gone before me and marked out this crazy path. They reminded me I was equipped and had everything I needed to do what God had called me to. And as I trusted Jesus in each new thing I had to learn or task I had to accomplish, I watched Him keep His promises.

In Isaiah 41:10 the Lord says: "Do not fear, for I am with you; do not be dismayed, for I am your God. I will strengthen you and help you; I will uphold you with my righteous right hand."

I have clung to this verse when life seems to be happening faster than I can keep up with. It's comforting to know that the same God who conquered death by raising His Son from the dead helps me through the ups and downs of life. No matter what I'm going through, He can handle it.

Maybe today you're walking through a season that feels a little shaky. Maybe you're facing a move or attending a new school. Maybe you've experienced a breakup or a shift in your friend group. Change can feel disorienting, like you're a plant being removed from one pot and planted in another. It's easy to become anxious or miss your old, comfortable flowerpot. But God uses those uncomfortable seasons to open new doors and stretch our faith in powerful ways.

Even when change is exciting, like stepping into a dream opportunity, we still need God's strength. During my first headlining tour, where I was the main act on stage night after night, I felt the weight of wanting to give my best and glorify God. I battled moments of doubt, wondering if I was in the right place. But every single time, God showed up and gave me exactly what I needed. The best part was meeting sweet fans, especially those from Hey Girl Nation. Night after night, the Lord gave me a special blessing through people who shared how my music helped them. If I'd let fear win, I would've missed that.

If you're in a season of change, lean into Jesus. He's steady when everything else is shifting. He's strengthening you and holding you through every high and low. Look for the little gifts He's placing in your path, such as people to encourage you or small acts of provision.

REPEAT AFTER ME:

"God strengthens me during times of transition."

Scripture of the Day

Trust in the Lord
with all your heart,
and do not lean on
your own understanding.
In all your ways acknowledge
him, and he will make
straight your paths.

—Proverbs 3:5–6 ESV

Note to Self

What is a transition you've experienced (a move, a new school, a new church, etc.)?

How did God meet you in the chaos or uncertainty?

List three gifts or opportunities that came from the transition.

1.

2.

3.

Hey, Girl! Let's Talk to God

God,

You are so strong and so good. Thank You for being with me during transitions and times of uncertainty. Thank You for strengthening me and holding me up. Thank You that I don't have to fear any change because You go ahead of me, with me, and behind me. You make my paths straight. Help me to trust You more deeply. Give me the strength and courage to keep going, and help me to see the gifts and opportunities You're providing, even in chaotic moments.

Amen.

DAY 35:

★ ★ ★

One of my favorite things about my brother, Jacob, was that he truly lived Jesus' words in Luke 6:45: "A good man brings good things out of the good stored up in his heart, and an evil man brings evil things out of the evil stored up in his heart. For the mouth speaks what the heart is full of." He never spoke an unkind word about anyone. If I started to veer into gossip or utter a critical word about someone, he'd stop me.

Jacob didn't just talk with kindness; he lived with kindness. He made people feel seen, valued, and welcomed. You could tell his good words weren't just a performance. Positive speech flowed out naturally from Jacob because his heart was full of the right things.

Jesus said something really powerful in Luke 6:45: Our words are an overflow of what's already in our hearts. If we're allowing God to cultivate goodness and grace inside us, it's going to spill out. But if we've let bitterness or pride take root, that's what will come up!

I've often thought, *I need to watch my mouth.* And self-control is a fruit of the Spirit. Sometimes I just need to bite my tongue. But the bigger issue is my mouth mirrors my heart. So if I want to speak love, hope, and encouragement, I must start by storing up those things in my heart.

I do that by spending time with Jesus, soaking up His Word, and allowing Him to shape my thinking. As He fills me, love, patience, and kindness will naturally flow out in my speech. Jacob was a wonderful example of that to me. He blessed others instead of cursing them. He encouraged instead of criticized. His heart was full of kindness and so were his words. That's the kind of person I want to be.

Our words are a direct reflection of what's in our hearts. If negative speech is regularly crossing your lips—criticism, complaint, swearing, or rude comments—maybe it's time to ask God to do heart surgery. In Ezekiel 36:26 He said, "I will give you a new heart and put a new spirit in you." As we allow Him to transform our hearts, our speech will follow… and so will our influence.

I've never forgotten my brother's example of kindness. It inspires me to speak words that honor the Lord and make others feel valued.

REPEAT AFTER ME:

"I can speak words from my heart that honor God and others."

Scripture of the Day

A good man brings good things out of the good stored up in his heart, and an evil man brings evil things out of the evil stored up in his heart. For the mouth speaks what the heart is full of.

—Luke 6:45

Note to Self

List some good qualities you would like to store up in your heart that might affect your speech. (Look up and read Galatians 5:22–23, Colossians 3:12, and 2 Peter 1:5–7 for ideas.)

Who is someone who has been an example of kind speech for you? What have they taught you?

Hey, Girl! Let's Talk to God

Heavenly Father,

Thank You for the power of words. I know what comes out of my mouth starts deep inside me. Cleanse my heart of bitterness, pride, anger, and any ungodly thing that needs to go. Thank You for promising to give me a new heart and fill me with Your Spirit. I pray my words would be an overflow of the love and kindness You are developing in me. Help me to be a woman with a pure heart who reflects You and sets an example for others.

In Jesus' precious name, amen.

SECTION EIGHT

Live Free, Walk in Victory

It is for freedom that Christ has set us free.
Stand firm, then, and do not
let yourselves be burdened again
by a yoke of slavery.

—Galatians 5:1

Freedom is such a powerful word. Jesus didn't just come to give us eternal life; He came to give us freedom and victory in our daily lives. Through His sacrifice on the cross, He freed us from our sin and shame. We don't have to be defined by the past or our performance. He invites us to stand firm in who He says we are—His chosen, loved, and forgiven daughters.

We no longer carry the weight of trying to earn our salvation because Jesus paid the price. Living free means letting go of the fear that holds us captive and asking God to help us be exactly who He made us to be.

Victory isn't just for the strong. It's for the broken, the hurting, and the healing. All of us have battle wounds that cause us to limp. True victory isn't found in striving to be good but in surrendering fully to the One who *is good*. We can walk in victory because Jesus already won the battle. You are free! Not just to survive but to live boldly and serve Jesus with everything you've got.

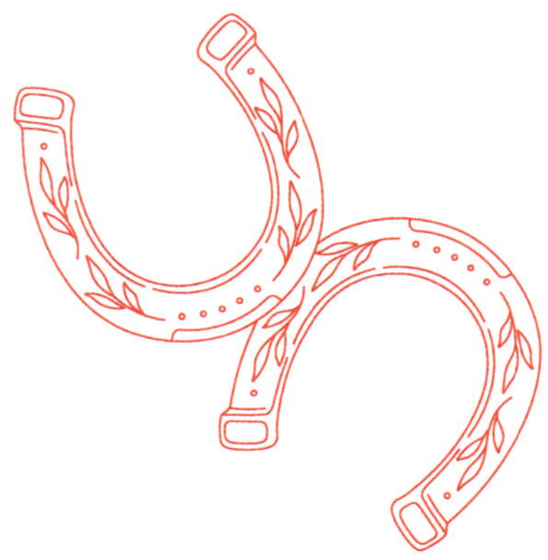

DAY 36:

Don't Forget You're Free

★ ★ ★

God's chosen people, the Israelites, knew captivity all too well. Over four hundred years before Jesus came to earth, they were taken into captivity by the Babylonians. They must have felt such heartbreak, living in a strange land, cut off from everything familiar and the freedom they once knew.

But even during a heartbreaking chapter of Israel's history, God was faithful. Even though His people suffered, He never broke His promises and He never abandoned them. The Babylonian exile lasted seventy long years, but it did end. The Israelites returned home. Just like God had done when He brought them out of Egypt, He made a way for them to return to their land. That's what our God does—He hears the cries of His people and responds with mercy.

While you and I may not be physically enslaved like the Israelites were, we all face things that threaten to hold us captive—sin, shame, anxiety, addiction. The enemy would love to keep us in chains. In fact, 1 Peter 5:8 warns us: "Your enemy the devil prowls around like a roaring lion looking for someone to devour."

Some chains are subtle, aren't they? Maybe you're not addicted to drugs, but you can't seem to scroll through Instagram without comparing your life to someone else's. Maybe you're not openly rebelling, but there's bitterness or unforgiveness that's keeping you stuck. God sees it all, and Jesus frees us.

In His Word, God says He will "proclaim freedom for the captives and release from darkness for the prisoners" (Isa. 61:1). Those words aren't only for the Israelites. They're also for us. Jesus came to fulfill that very promise. He bled and died so we wouldn't have to live shackled by past mistakes or held captive by lies from the enemy.

I love something I heard a youth pastor say: "Condemnation pushes us away from God, but conviction pulls us closer." God doesn't want us to sit in the destruction our sin has caused. Instead, He pulls us close to be healed and experience freedom.

Some days we're a lot like the Israelites, aren't we? We feel trapped in our circumstances—pain, betrayal, or conditions we didn't ask for or want. At times, we walk into the prison ourselves, choosing sin over obedience. But no matter how we got there, God never leaves us in chains. His plan has always been to free us, restore us, and remind us of who we are—loved and chosen daughters of the King.

When Jesus died on the cross, He paid the price for all our sins—past, present, and future. He broke every chain and opened every prison door. That's the Jesus we serve!

If you feel like you're stuck in a place with little hope for the future, God sees beyond your limited vision. He's writing your story, and He doesn't make mistakes. You might be on a hard page right now, but the next chapter holds healing, joy, and freedom. So don't give up. Jesus bought your freedom, and the Holy Spirit helps you to walk in it.

REPEAT AFTER ME:

"Jesus proclaims freedom in my life
and the Holy Spirit helps me walk in it."

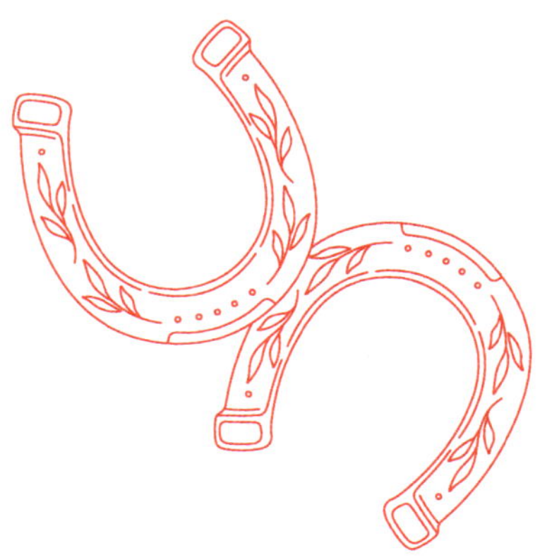

Scripture of the Day

Now the Lord
is the Spirit,
and where the
Spirit of the Lord is,
there is freedom.

—2 Corinthians 3:17

In what areas of life do you feel held captive (sin, insecurity, hard circumstances, past mistakes, etc.)?

What do you need to ask Jesus to free you from?

What would this next week look like if you walked fully in the freedom Christ died to give you?

Hey, Girl! Let's Talk to God

Lord,

Thank You for loving me so much that You paid the ultimate price to give me freedom and make my heart whole. You don't want me to be enslaved to anything—other people's opinions, fear and anxiety, selfishness, pride, or addictions. I confess that I've sometimes walked back into the prison and allowed myself to be held captive. Lord, I ask for Your freedom today. Allow me to walk in freedom and truth through Your Spirit.

In Jesus' beautiful name, amen.

DAY 37:

When Life Falls Apart

★ ★ ★

Have you ever had a season where it felt like everything was going wrong and you were taking one hit after another? Just a few months after my brother, Jacob, went to heaven, my family and I entered what we now call our "Job season." Perhaps you're familiar with Job in the Bible. Life was good for Job until suddenly, he lost his wealth, his livestock, his children, and his health. Even Job's wife said, "Curse God and die!" (Job 2:9).

We didn't lose everything like Job did, but it felt like it. Our hearts were already broken from losing Jacob. Then a pipe burst in our bathroom and flooded the house so badly that the ceiling caved in. We had to move into a hotel for six weeks right before school started. Not long after that, my dad lost his job, my mom got shingles, and I broke my arm so badly I needed surgery. It felt like we couldn't catch a break.

Our emotional reserves were drained, and we kept getting hit with a new form of trouble. I tried to surrender it all into God's hands, but beneath the surface I worried my strength would give out if just one more thing went wrong.

But in the chaos and the pain, God was present. He didn't leave. He didn't abandon us. Sometimes we go through seasons that don't make sense and feel impossible to endure. The apostle Paul understood this and wrote about it in 2 Corinthians 12:9–10. Speaking of the Lord, Paul wrote: "But he said to me, 'My grace is sufficient for you, for my power is made perfect in weakness.' Therefore I will boast all the more gladly about my weaknesses, so that Christ's power may rest on me. That is why, for Christ's sake, I delight in weaknesses, in insults, in hardships, in persecutions, in difficulties. For when I am weak, then I am strong."

That's such a powerful promise when life seems to be falling apart and we don't have the strength to go on. God will carry us in those moments and His power will be made perfect in our weakness. That's a truth I've had to cling to many times in my life. His grace is enough!

If you're in your own "Job season," hold on. Your suffering won't last forever; joy comes in the morning (Ps. 30:5). Job's story had a happy ending—God restored his fortune and gave him twice as much as he had before (Job 42:10). When you feel like you can't take another step, draw on God's grace. He sees the full picture and will give you all the strength you need to walk in victory.

REPEAT AFTER ME:

"God is with me in my suffering."

Scripture of the Day

After you have
suffered for a little while,
the God of all grace,
who called you to His
eternal glory in Christ,
will Himself perfect,
confirm, strengthen,
and establish you.

—1 Peter 5:10 NASB

Talk about a "Job season" in your own life. How was God present in your suffering? Where did His grace show up?

Read Job 42:10–17. How did Job's story end? What does this reveal about God's character and how does it give you hope?

Write 1 Peter 5:10 on several index cards and place them in your room, around your home, or in your locker to remind you that suffering is temporary.

Hey, Girl! Let's Talk to God

All-Knowing God,

Thank You for being with me in "Job seasons." Thank You for Your promise to never abandon me and the grace You give me when it feels like my strength is gone. Your power is made perfect in my weakness, and I pray that You would be glorified through me in my suffering. May my troubles point others to You. I trust You, my Jesus. Thank You for the hope of Your eternal glory.

Amen.

DAY 38:

Shame Long Gone

★ ★ ★

Shame has always been a struggle for me. I remember moments as a teenager when someone's passing comment about my weight would pierce deeper than they could've imagined. Not to mention how hard I was on myself! In my imperfection I felt unworthy, like I didn't measure up. That shame led me to isolate myself, and ironically, I turned to food for comfort—which only deepened the cycle and made me feel worse.

Shame is sneaky like that. It whispers, *You're not enough. You're broken beyond repair.* That voice can easily grow louder than the truth because shame is a weapon of the enemy. Shame not only drives a wedge between us and God—who accepts us fully just as we are—it also isolates us from others. Shame tries to convince us that we're the only one who has messed up so badly, and we're too flawed to be loved or accepted.

The truth is, none of us measure up—not perfectly, anyway. Romans 3:23 says, "For all have sinned and fall short of the glory of God." When we come face-to-face with our sin, there's a necessary moment of recognizing our guilt, and that Jesus died to pay the price for our sins. But *guilt* and *shame* are different. Guilt says, "I did something wrong." Shame says, "I am something wrong." And that's where Satan, God's enemy, tries to twist the truth.

I've wrestled with that distinction for years. I've sat in silence after sin, not just feeling remorse but believing I was unlovable because of my sin. I've compared myself to others, convinced I wasn't good enough to be used by God. Can you relate?

The truth is, shame is not of God. His Spirit convicts us of our sin, yes. But His conviction is filled with hope and freedom because Jesus paid for that sin in full. Isaiah 50:7 says, "Because the Sovereign Lord helps me, I will not be disgraced. Therefore have I set my face like flint, and I know I will not be put to shame." That verse has become an anchor for me. When lies from the enemy rise up, telling me I'm not worthy, I remind myself that God doesn't shame His children; He clothes them in righteousness.

When I've returned to God after seasons of shame, I've felt embarrassed, thinking, *I can't come to You in this condition.* But God welcomes a contrite heart (Ps. 51:17); He loves humility. He doesn't ask us to clean ourselves up first. He just wants us to run into His arms.

If you're carrying shame today, remember that Jesus bore your shame on the cross. He took our sin and shame so we don't have to. You don't need to hide in the shadows or prove your worth. You are already deeply loved, fully known, and covered by His grace.

So take off the cloak of shame and let Him dress you in His righteousness. Remember that because of Jesus' sacrifice, your shame is long gone. I'm still learning to let go, but every step toward Jesus is a step away from shame. No matter what you've done or what your past looks like, you're not beyond His reach. Set your face like flint and walk boldly into the freedom He's already won for you.

REPEAT AFTER ME:

"I can let go of my shame
and walk in Christ's righteousness."

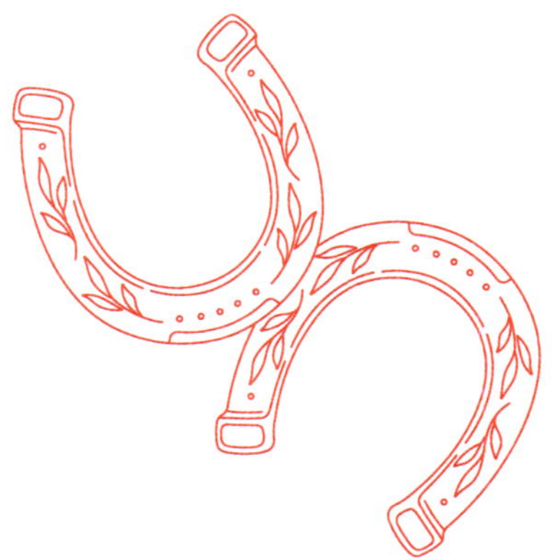

Scripture of the Day

Do not be afraid;
you will not be
put to shame.
Do not fear disgrace;
you will not be humiliated.
You will forget the
shame of your youth.

—Isaiah 54:4

Note to Self

Think of some areas of shame in your life (body image, past mistakes, failing to meet expectations, sin struggles, etc.). List them here.

Now surrender your shame to God, remembering that Jesus paid the full price for your sin—past, present, and future. He is inviting you to drop your shame and move forward in His love.

One way the enemy keeps us bound by shame is through the lie "I'm the only one." Read James 5:16. Think of one or more trusted, spiritually mature people with whom you can share your struggles. Write down their names.

Bringing things into the light releases the grip of shame. What is one step toward Jesus and away from shame you can take this week?

Hey, Girl! Let's Talk to God

Lord of Mercy,

Thank You for taking my shame to the cross and clothing me in Your righteousness. So often I listen to the lies telling me that I'm not enough or that I'm a failure. But Your blood speaks a better word over me. You call me *chosen*, *beloved*, *redeemed*. Help me remember that guilt is meant to lead me to repentance, not to a place of hiding. Remind me that shame is not from You and that I don't have to earn Your love. When I feel like I can't come to You in my mess, remind me that You welcome me just as I am. Strengthen me to walk in the truth of who I am and help me live fully in Your freedom.

In Jesus' name, amen.

DAY 39:

★ ★ ★

Have you ever wondered who you really are? Like, who has God created you to be? How will you contribute to this world He's put you in?

When I first became a music artist, I learned I would need to settle on a distinct sound and style. Everyone seemed to have ideas about what that sound should be, but none of their suggestions felt right to me. One day I wrestled with this decision at my grandad's farm, a place where I did some of my best thinking and praying. *Jesus,* I prayed, *You placed me on this journey, and I trust You to lead me in it. Please show me the unique sound You've given me.*

I'd lost my brother, Jacob, three years earlier, and I wished he was there to give me advice. Wanting to feel close to him, I turned up some country music on my phone. I was transported back to Friday afternoons riding shotgun in my big brother's truck, listening to the familiar music.

That's when it dawned on me—I was a Southern girl whose heart's desire was to worship Jesus. *What if country music and worship music collided?* I thought. I suddenly knew—*that* was my sound.

With my second album, *Rebel*, I was encouraged to release songs on country music radio as well as Christian radio. I was hesitant, because I didn't want to change who I was. I wanted to stay true to both my Southern roots and love of country music, and my Christian beliefs and desire to worship. I was relieved to be told, "We want you to be exactly who you are." I would be free to share the love of Jesus in country music.

I realized that all my life God had been preparing me to be this kind of artist: a girl from the South, singing about Jesus and wanting to honor her brother's memory. I love how specific Jesus is with each of His children. With me, He brought two kinds of music together—and gave me an unusual path to being an artist—all for the purpose of sharing Him with others.

I love the words of Ephesians 2:10, "For we are God's handiwork, created in Christ Jesus to do good works, which God prepared in advance for us to do." The original Greek word for "handiwork" in this passage is *poema*, the root word for our English word *poem*, and means a work of art.[3] I am a piece of art created in Christ Jesus to do good works He planned for me before I was born. God's intentionality is next level, y'all.

Have you found your "sound"? What do you feel made to do? Maybe God has created you to be an encourager. Perhaps He's given you a heart for unity. Or maybe you lead others to be their best. Think of it this way: If the work God has you do is the car, your purpose is the gasoline. Singing and writing songs are my car; telling people about my Jesus is the gas.

While my story (and probably yours) has many twists and turns, God used each experience to make me the person I am today *so that* I could accomplish the work He has for me. Your life experiences are not a coincidence. Each relationship and experience is a line in the poem God is writing in your life. Praise Him today for not just creating you but *crafting you* for His glory.

REPEAT AFTER ME:

"I am a work of art created in Christ Jesus to do good works."

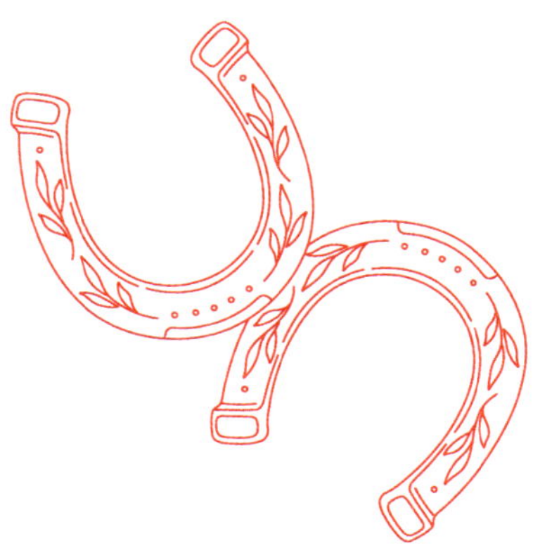

Scripture of the Day

For we are God's
handiwork, created in
Christ Jesus to do
good works,
which God
prepared in advance
for us to do.

—Ephesians 2:10

Note to Self

What is your "sound"? List some of the passions and abilities that make you who you are. How might God use these for His glory?

How does it make you feel to know that you are a piece of art created by God to do good works?

What are some good works God may have for you this week? (Examples: to encourage a friend, to help a neighbor, to use your talents to bless someone, etc.)

Hey, Girl! Let's Talk to God

Lord of Mercy,

Thank You for designing and building me to be exactly who I am. How amazing that You care so deeply about the details of my life! Thank You for using even my painful experiences to shape me and prepare me for the good works You have for me to accomplish. Your wisdom in creation is beyond my comprehension. Today I offer all that I am to You. Use me, Lord!

In the precious name of Jesus, amen.

DAY 40:

Breathtaking View

★ ★ ★

I'll never forget one particular bike ride with Jacob. It was a holy moment tucked into an ordinary summer vacation. At the time, I didn't know it would be one of our last adventures together. I didn't know I'd hold on to the memory forever, replaying each moment in my mind.

It was a beautiful evening in Florida. As the sun painted the sky pink and orange, and the waves quietly brushed the shore, Jacob and I stood still in the presence of something greater than ourselves. I would later learn that he had scouted out that spot days before and timed it perfectly so we could be there together just as the sun lit the sky with its final glory. I will never forget that moment.

On our way to that spot, I'd questioned where my brother was taking me and if my legs would hold out for the ride. A planner by nature, I was impatient with the long, uncharted journey.

It makes me think about how sometimes in our lives, we feel like we're on a ride we don't understand. The road is longer than we thought it would be, our legs burn from exertion, and we question if the destination is worth the effort.

"How much longer?" we ask. And God whispers, *Just a bit farther.*

Then, without warning, the path opens up to something breathtaking—a view you couldn't have imagined. That's how God leads us—with love, grace, and purpose. Like Jacob's elaborate route to that beach (it took a miracle for me to find that beach again!), God knows exactly where He's taking us—even when we have no clue.

When we come to hard or seemingly impassable points in the journey, He promises to be with us and give us peace beyond understanding (Phil. 4:7). At the hardest points in my life, I've experienced that indescribable peace as I just keep pedaling.

Maybe today you feel confused or discouraged. The path you're on feels too long, too hard, or too painful. Remember that God is leading you somewhere more beautiful than you could imagine. Jacob gave me a glimpse of that with that unforgettable bike ride, which is one of my most treasured memories. I now know that every turn in the road has purpose, so we should never give up. The ride may be long, but the view at the end will take your breath away.

REPEAT AFTER ME:

"God is leading me somewhere
more beautiful than I could imagine."

Scripture of the Day

Many are
the plans in
a person's heart,
but it is the
Lord's purpose
that prevails.

—Proverbs 19:21

Note to Self

Think of a time when something beautiful came out of something hard. What happened? How did God give you more than you were expecting?

How have you experienced God's peace in the unknowns of life? How does His love and care inspire you to trust Him more?

Hey, Girl! Let's Talk to God

Loving Father,

Thank You for creating me with a purpose and being by my side on this journey through life. When the path feels long, help me to trust that You're leading me somewhere beautiful. Thank You for the glimpses of heaven You give along the way, and for the people who remind me of Your deep love for me. Give me Your peace today and help me to trust You more.

In Your Son's precious name, amen.

Acknowledgments

★ ★ ★

When I look back over the past five years, I am amazed to see all God has done. One of my greatest joys has been founding "Hey Girl Nation," a movement and community for women of all ages to embrace the message of the song—that we can feel valuable and empowered exactly as we are because our worth is found in Christ. I'm so grateful for the team of people the Lord has surrounded me with, who have offered love, encouragement, and support to make this devotional possible.

Thank you to my precious family—my dad, Kent, and my beautiful sister, Elizabeth—you have encouraged me, supported me, and inspired me through this process. Thank you to my mom, Lynn, for helping shape me into the woman I am today, being a praying mama, and always pointing me back to Jesus. And thank you to my precious brother in heaven, Jacob. Your legacy of love and faithfulness continues to live on in everything I do. I am so grateful for the time I had with you. I miss you every day.

Thank you to Erica McDonald for mentoring me and inspiring me to be a woman of God.

Thank you to my manager, Matthew West, and the team at Story House Collective for helping make this dream project a reality! And thank you, Matthew and Jeff Pardo, for sharing my vision for the song "Hey Girl" and helping me write it. That song has had a greater impact than any of us imagined.

Special thanks to Suzanne Gosselin for partnering with me on this devotional and helping me put the messages in my heart onto the pages. Marcie Maggart, thank you for once again bringing your excellence and wisdom to this project. I am grateful for you.

Thank you to K-LOVE Books Vice President of Publishing Karen Longino and Sr. Publishing Manager Jenaye Merida for giving me the opportunity to expand the reach of "Hey Girl" through this book. Your encouragement and support have been a blessing.

Thank you to all the "Hey Girls" out there who are pursuing Jesus and going deeper with Him. It has been my joy and privilege to meet so many of you at my concerts and hear your stories. You inspire me! I hope this book will inspire you to walk in the freedom of your true identity as a blood-bought, battle-fought, made-new child of the King!

Finally, thank You to my Jesus who loves me and has done immeasurably more than I asked or imagined (Eph. 3:20). All of this is for You. I love You.

About the Author

★ ★ ★

Anne Wilson grew up in Kentucky with her parents and two siblings, Elizabeth and Jacob. Her family's Christian faith sustained them through the tragic loss of Jacob when he was only 23 years old. She has become an award-winning singer and songwriter, garnering multiple honors. Along with a fervor for writing and singing songs that draw others to Jesus, Anne is passionate about helping young women embrace their identity in Christ and discover His purposes for their lives. In 2022 she founded the online community "Hey Girl Nation" to spread that message and remind girls of their worth in Him. Anne loves meeting with "Hey Girls" at every concert.

1. Jess Whitley, "The Life of Amy Carmichael," Girl Got Faith, August 11, 2017, https://girlgotfaith.com/2017/08/11/the-life-of-amy-charmichael/.

2. Felicia Czochanski Bisaro, "3 Real-Life, Jaw-Dropping Lucky Finds at Goodwill," Goodwill, accessed May 13, 2025, https://www.goodwill.org/blog/shop/3-real-life-jaw-dropping-lucky-finds-at-goodwill/.

3. "Breakout Singer-Songwriter Anne Wilson Scores Her First RIAA Gold Certification for Her Hit Single, 'My Jesus,'" Capitol Christian Music Group, May 9, 2022, https://www.capitolcmglabelgroup.com/news/breakout-singer-songwriter-anne-wilson-scores-her-first-riaa-gold-certification-her-hit-single/.

4. John Newton, "Amazing Grace," Hymnary, https://hymnary.org/text/amazing_grace_how_sweet_the_sound. Public domain.

5. "Poiēma," *Blue Letter Bible*, https://www.blueletterbible.org/lexicon/g4161/kjv/tr/0-1/.

★ ★ ★

★ ★ ★

★ ★ ★

★ ★ ★

★ ★ ★

★ ★ ★

JOIN HEY GIRL NATION TODAY!

A COMMUNITY OF PRAYER & ENCOURAGEMENT THAT EMPOWERS YOU TO BE WHO GOD MADE YOU TO BE!

FOLLOW ALONG ON SOCIALS!

@heygirlnation
@annewilsonmusic

heygirlnation.com   annewilsonofficial.com

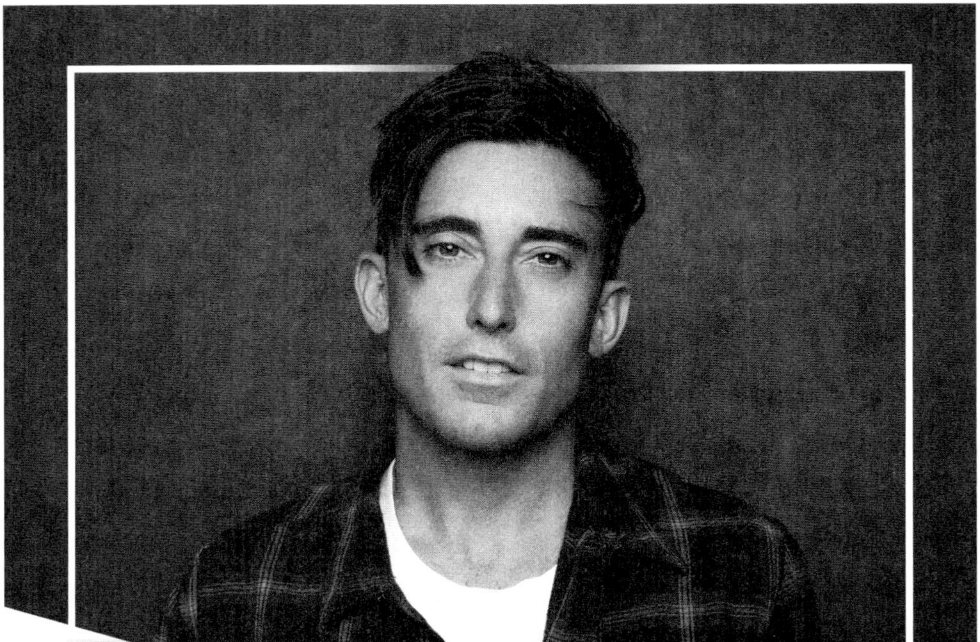

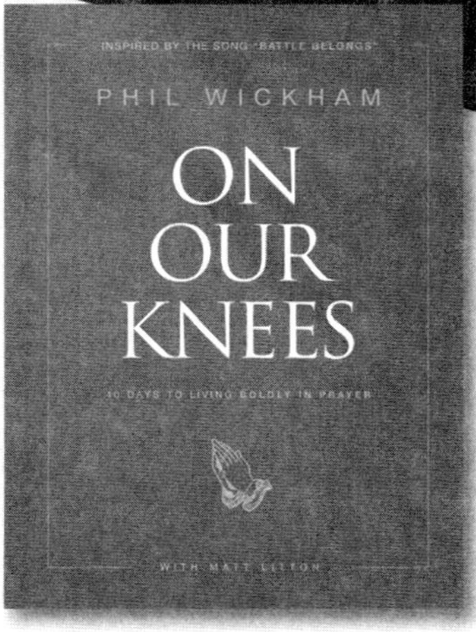
INSPIRED BY THE SONG "BATTLE BELONGS"
PHIL WICKHAM
ON OUR KNEES

YOU ARE SEEN, LOVED,
AND MADE FOR MORE